OCEAN NOMAD

OCEAN NOMAD

My Life – R778537

Eddie Bolton

PENSION FUND AND REGISTERED No.	
NATIONAL INSURANCE NUMBER YH/31/32/76 C	UNION OR SOCIETY Name...... NUS No. 359004

GRADE NUMBER
AND DATE OF ISSUE OF CERTIFICATES OF COMPETENCY HELD

DECLARATION.

I DECLARE (i) that the person to whom this Discharge Book relates has satisfied me that he (she) is a seaman and (ii) that the photograph affixed bearing my official stamp is a true likeness of that person, that the signature within is his (her) true signature, that he (she) possesses the physical characteristics entered within and has stated to me the date and place of his (her) birth as entered within.

SIGNATURE OF SUPT. AT
MERCANTILE MARINE OFFICE—

_____

DATE _____

R 77853 7

M.M.O. EMBOSSING STAMP

Dedication

I would like to dedicate this book to my parents who brought me up to the true values of life and respect to other people, also to my brother and sisters. I would like to share it with all my seafaring friends whom I had the privilege to have sailed with and known over the years. Without them it would not have been the same. They know who I mean, especially the men I sailed with as a young boy, who themselves had sailed the convoys of the Second World War. They taught me discipline and respect for others. Also to the ones who have crossed the bar and to my friends here in the UK not forgetting all my very good friends in Australia and New Zealand, who made our voyages down there more memorable and worthwhile. And the other places around the World.

There are places I remember, in my life I have seen them all

John Winston Lennon

Contents

Chapter 1
Beginnings

I was born in January 1947 along with my twin sister Ruth who was born an hour before me. She was named after my mother. I was named after my father, Albert Edward, but I was named Edward Albert to avoid any confusion! My father was from London and he met my mother in 1940 when he was stationed in Aintree, Liverpool, whilst in the army waiting to go overseas. War had been declared in 1939, although Germany, Italy and Japan had not yet come in to this war on the side of the Axis. My father was to spend the next five years in the Middle East fighting alongside other regiments against the Italians and Rommel's African corps in Tobruk and Abyssinia, then on to the Burma campaign against the Japanese with the Chindit Special forces in 1944 under Wingate. Before he died he wrote an account of his experience throughout both theatres of the war up to his coming home and marrying my mother. My mother had another baby girl before she had us, but the child died soon after birth – a different story which I will explain later.

I was born in an old Victorian house which my grandmother and grandfather lived in close to the docks and the city centre, an area populated mainly by Irish and Italian immigrants, large families who did not have a lot of possessions. It was a really close-knit community that helped each other out in difficult times. You could leave your door open and not worry about thieves, vandalism or anti-social behaviour. It was not like it is today and sadly these wonderful people are gone. A lot of the families split up after the war, some by past events such as losing loved ones in the war or to diseases like tuberculosis.

My grandmother lost four of her ten children. She went through hard times but remained strong. I think the birth of my sister and I helped her through her loss. She was a wonderful grandmother of Irish stock. She herself was from a big family. I remember all of her sisters, they were always visiting. They used to say I was her 'blue eye'. I remember as a child her buying me sweets and ice cream. She was the type of woman who would not leave anyone out so she would buy ice cream for all the other kids in the street. As I grew older I went to visit her every Sunday. I would get the bus from Childwall to T G Hughes shop where I would get off and walk down Stafford Street to Upper Beau Street, where she lived. She would also visit us at the prefab in Childwall, bringing us bags of fruit and sweets. They were some of the happiest times of my life.

My gran had six girls and four boys: two of the girls had died before I was born and two of the boys Jimmy and Eddie died when I was born – Eddie from heart disease and Jimmy from TB after serving in the Gordon Highland Regiment at the Salerno landing in Italy during the Second World War. I always remember my grandmother telling me of her son's words about us being born. "Mam," he said, "there is another baby coming," He was overjoyed that his sister was having twins. He took ill soon after and died.

After her son received invalid pay from the army, my grandmother used to go up to Scotland where he was in a military hospital. Her family were very devout Roman Catholics and the church was everything to them. My sister and I were christened in St Mary of the Angels RC Church in Fox Street by Franciscan Monks. The church is still there to this day but is no longer in use, like many of the churches today. Sadly, all of the older people are no longer with us and their families have moved on, and the remaining people do not bother with the church. It is a different generation today, when you think back to all those big families that had weddings, funerals and christenings there.

The old houses no longer stand there, it is now waste ground. I often go out of my way and look at the church and the street where I was born and picture my childhood days and think about all the people I knew in the street. The only thing that still stands at the end of the street is the old leather works. Although it is no longer in use, it is a listed building, along with the church. A lot of the houses in the street were destroyed during the bombings in the Second World War.

We lived in my grandmother's house with my mother and father in a small room, along with my aunties and uncles. There must have been seven of us along with my grandfather, brother and my mother's uncle Peter. Peter had no home so my grandmother took him in. He was a kind old man who smoked a pipe. I used to love the smell of tobacco from the pipe. I recall him taking me out for the day over the river Mersey on the ferry boat. I was only six but I have a really good memory for certain things in my past. I can remember being terrified of the water and would not go near the ferry rails or look over into the river. Funny really when you think that I spent my life from the age of 15 to 67 at sea travelling the world – more of which later!

I remember my auntie Marge, my mum's younger sister, getting married in the 1950s in the same church as I was born and having the reception in grandmother's house. One of the things I do remember was this older man with his face blackened with boot polish and a turban-like thing on his head, dancing and singing and everyone clapping him. I remember asking my dad why he was all blacked up. Apparently he was a boy soldier in the Zulu wars in the late 1890s and he was imitating one of the Zulu dances, not showing any form of disrespect but more in respect. Imagine the uproar it would cause with today's political correctness?

Francis, my mother's younger brother, was out in Malaysia doing his national service. He was my Nan's youngest son. She had him late on in life. Joseph, or Joey, was mum's other brother who had married Nelly and was living in St Andrews Gardens, a huge block of tenements known as the Bull Ring, along with those wonderful people that you very rarely see nowadays. The tenements are still there today but are now used as student's accommodation. For some reason they moved out all those families to other parts of Liverpool, splitting up the good families and characters which used to live there. My uncle Joey was one of those characters – he was well known and respected by everyone in Liverpool. He later went on to have five children.

My uncle Frank never married, remaining a bachelor like myself, and died in late 1980. He was a great man and character. He should have been a comedian. Uncle Eddie was married and died towards the end of 1940. He had two children but I never saw much of them, as his wife remarried and lost touch with the families. Margie, who I spoke of, married Freddie Newton (another lovely man) and had three girls and a boy. Unfortunately Freddie died in the 1960s. He was in ill-health and had chest problems. He would probably have survived longer with modern medicine. Collette, Maria, Margaret and Paul were Margie's children, and sadly Margaret died at a young age from a brain tumour. She was a lovely girl. Margie had a lot of tragedy in her life, losing her brothers and sisters and then her husband and daughter. But she kept strong in her faith and loved her church. I think that kept her going until she passed away in the 1990s at 68.

Auntie Annie, Mum's other sister, married Christy O'Donohue and had two girls and two boys. Annie was a lovely person as was Christy. She died in the 1980s. Christy is still alive today, along with his children, my cousins. I don't know much about Winnie and Mary, my aunties who died before I was born, but I remember my mother talking about them. I will come to my father's side of the family later on.

Chapter 2
Moving Out to Childwall

Like all men who came home from the war, my father had to settle down to civilian life, having seen action in the western desert and Burma. He was away for four years and was only a young lad.

My earliest recollection is waking up on Christmas Day in the prefab and playing with toys. We moved there in about 1950. My sister and I were about three years old when we had to leave my nans house as my mother's sister, Annie, still lived at Nan's and was about to have her own family. Margie was not married and Frank was a young boy and Joey still lived there. My mother was both sad and overjoyed to move as the prefab was a house built after the war. Rather like a bungalow, with two bedrooms, toilet, cooker and boiler in the kitchen with fitted cupboards made of iron, a hallway, bathroom and living room. Really modern I would say for that time. It also had a garden back and front with a coal shed at the side. There were hundreds of them built all over, and we happened to be right out in the country surrounded by land and farms miles from the city. They were to be the happiest days of mum's life and my own.

It was very difficult for my father finding a job along with most ex-service men at that time. Although, in spite of my father's London accent, he eventually got one as a lorry driver as he'd learned to drive in the army. He enlisted at 18 years of age. He was well liked by everyone and had a kind and considerate nature.

When I was older my nan used to tell me about my dad coming to the house before he went overseas to war, standing outside waiting to see my mother as they began courting. "Come in whoever you are," she shouted to him with that welcome you rarely see today. That was my dad's first introduction to the Sullivan family, the beginning of a relationship that would last for a long time. The second time was when my father came home from Burma having been to see his own family in a place called Watford, where they first lived before moving to London. He walked down the street in his uniform and Australian slouch hat worn by the chindits to see my mother. They had kept in touch throughout the war. Everybody had a rough time during the war, with the constant air raids, the German bombers causing everyone to rush in to the air raid shelters, but they came through it all. People think they have it hard today but thinking of what they went through in the war years with rations and houses bombed, yet they still maintained that sense of togetherness and community spirit – it is unimaginable nowadays.

Dad's family lived in London and he had been born in East End Bow. His father was a Londoner and his mother, my gran, was born in Cardiff, South Wales. She was of Irish stock too, and Conner was her name before she married my granddad. My dad was the eldest of five with four sisters, three of whom are still alive today. Their names were Annie, Doreen, Kathleen, and Margaret the youngest died recently. She married an American airman in the 1950s and had two boys. She lived in America until she died. I remember Margaret well. When my dad came home and knocked on the door of his mother's she answered and said, "Mum, there's an Australian soldier at the door." She was only young when he went to war. Soon after returning he went up to Liverpool where he met Mum and made it his home until he died. He was buried in Allerton cemetery with our mum.

I can remember my first day at school along with my sister. The name of the school was Joseph Williams Church of England School – that was in 1952, as there was not a Catholic school built, but the headmaster let us R.C. kids attend religious instructions in our local church, Our Lady of Assumption. We all mixed well and no bigotry existed with us kids – not like Northern Ireland where kids had their own schools and R.C. and Protestant never mixed. It was so sad really, not their fault. To be honest I don't think they should have different schools for other religions, they should all be one school mixed together. Then when they get older, let them decide what they want to do.

My school days were happy – no trouble, us kids played together, although I did not like everyday school. It had its ups and downs, but it taught me to respect people and my parents, and for that I am truly grateful to this day. I remember answering my mother back one day and my father gave my sister a letter to give to the headmaster. I remember him well as a very strict man, immaculately dressed in a suit, waistcoat and pocket watch. I think I was ten years old and little did I know what was in the letter. Next thing I knew I was called out of class to the headmaster's study. "I have a letter from your father about you being cheeky to your mother," he said. He had told him to punish me. I received a real telling off and two strokes of the cane on my hand. I soon learnt my lesson not to back-chat my parents. It was the first and last time I ever did. Imagine today. Well, they are not allowed to use a cane today if a child or a pupil misbehaves. They run home to the parents and the parents go up to the school wanting to know why you told their child off. Discipline begins at home from an early age and should keep up through to you leaving school. You become a better person really for your life ahead. We are not all angels, but I believe I am a better person for having a strict background. I look back on my early experiences which undoubtedly prepared me for my adult life.

The years I spent at Joseph Williams; the school holidays going fishing, out to the farms, playing football, a lot of friends and all good neighbours – they say your school days are the happiest days of your life. I left Joseph Williams School to go to the new Catholic school just built in 1959.

Before I go into that time, my brother James had been born in 1950 and then my mother had a little girl, Kathleen. I don't remember James being born but I remember my dad saying to me, "Go in and see your new little sister." My mother was in bed holding Kathleen. They were both born in the prefab. A lot of kids were born in the house in those days and a nurse used to come out to deliver the babies. Don't forget we never had central heating or fitted carpets, just a paraffin oil stove full of fumes and oil cloth blankets and army coats thrown over us in the winter time to keep warm. We did have a coal fire but it only gave off heat in the living room – lovely and warm until it was time for bed. Lighting the fire was to become my job when I was twelve, before I went out on my paper round at 6.30 in the morning before school. Before my sister was born Mum had a little girl named Anne, but sadly she died when she was a few weeks old.

My dad was out at 5.00am so had no time to light the fire. So I did it, first with paper, wood and then coal to get it going. Then I would go out to deliver my papers along the prefab. That was my first ever job. I used to give my mother half of my wages from the paper round as I had two jobs and the money was good – it all helped out. My father was a long distance lorry driver.

My years at Our Lady of Assumption School were happy. I made a lot of friends. My first teacher was a nun, Sister Francis. She was an ordinary teacher first, then she came back to the class as a nun in the summer holidays. I used to go and stay with my Dad's mother and father, granny and grandfather Bolton, in Watford just outside London. I stayed with her sometimes and dad's elder sister Annie who had two sons – one of my own age, Michael, and Gerald. Their dad was Jack Collar, a very quiet and gentle man. They were good to me and I had some of the best times of my life there and made a lot of friends. I had a job selling papers at Watford football ground. I still keep in touch with the Collars.

I never had any qualifications when I left school as I never paid much attention. I loved history, geography and football – that's about all – I hated maths. On Sundays I used to go over to the docks in Birkenhead, where you could get in easy as there were no gates like there were in Liverpool. I loved going to see all the ships coming in from all over the world and I used to say one day I will go away to sea.

I left school at 15 and first tried to get into the Royal Navy but failed the medical as I can only see out of one eye – a defect from birth. So I applied for the Merchant Navy and I got my first job as a cabin boy on a small coaster going to Belfast from Liverpool. I got a telegram to join it in Trafalgar Dock, Liverpool. I was thrilled but my father would not let me go at first, but he then signed the form for me to go.

I remember him taking me down to the ship in the car – it was August 1962, a Friday – I remember it well. When I got on board I had to report to the cook and when he first saw me he said, "Shouldn't you be at school?" My bag with my clothes in was bigger than me. I soon settled in and my job was keeping the mess room clean and doing the captain's cabin. The crew were all from Belfast and all tough seamen. I got on well with them all. The other cabin boy was from a place outside Belfast called Hollywood. His name was Gerry McCausland. He was a good friend and had a lovely family. Captain Miller who was strict but fair. One of my jobs was to get him two bottles of dandelion and burdock drink and a 20-pack of *Park Drive* cigarettes. I got on well with him and it was him who got me away to deep sea (foreign-going) after I left the *Buffalo* which was the name of my first ship.

We used to work a week on and three days off, and the money was really good. In those days I could earn up to £15 a week which was a lot of money for a boy of 15 back then. I paid ten shilling a week for my food, which was very good. The cook's name was John but the lads called him Joan! It took me a while for it to sink in but he never bothered us boys – he was in a world of his own but he was a good cook and clean. I was on her for one year and had some happy times on that ship. It gave me the experience to go to deep sea. I learned a lot from the older seamen about the sea, as well as respect and discipline. I remember them telling me the money from deep seafaring was not as good as you earned there – how right, as I was to find out.

Going across the Irish Sea in winter time could be rough and I used to get sea-sick, but you get used to it. After about six months the ship went to dry dock in Glasgow. I enjoyed my time up there – a lovely city and great people. It was there I met a lovely girl named Kathy Garrity who used to write to me, but I then moved on, as you do. Glasgow was a busy port with ships coming and going in different places over the world. There were so many British shipping companies then that you could practically pick where you wanted to go – anywhere in the world. Container ships had not yet emerged at that time.

After around three weeks in dry dock the ship sailed for Liverpool to continue our run for Belfast. We passed *Harland and Wolf* shipyards which held stocks of ships awaiting construction. 1963 came and the captain called me up to say that they had got me a job with the Blue Funnel Line, and that I had to go for a medical. I was worried in case I failed because of my eyesight, but to my delight the doctor passed me (thanks to Captain Miller and the chief mate who obviously held some influence). So the time came for me to say my goodbyes to the crew I had been with for twelve months. It was a sad day for me as I enjoyed being on that ship for so long. I can still remember most of the crew's names to this day, 53 years on. No doubt a lot of them will no longer be here with us today.

The Blue Funnel Line was one of the biggest companies in the country with its head office in India Buildings, Liverpool. I was soon to learn that I was to join a ship called the *Menestheus*. All the ships were named after Greek Gods. They had a regular liner service out to the Far East via the Suez Canal and also the Australian run from Liverpool. All the ships going to the Far East loaded and sailed from Birkenhead and returned and discharged in Liverpool. They then went around the coast discharging cargo and then loading them back to Birkenhead to finish off.

It was there I joined the *Menestheus* on a Saturday morning, 24th August 1963, to sail out to the Far East as a cabin boy. I was 16. I worked on the ship for a week before we sailed, cleaning and getting ready for sea. I was to be away for nearly four months. I found it a big difference to the crew on the *Buffalo*.

We sailed from Birkenhead and it took us three days to get to Gibraltar, where the weather was warming up after the grey skies and dark green seas, becoming beautiful blue sky and ocean. Gibraltar was lovely to see from the ship. We also passed the Queen Mary passenger ship before turning into the Mediterranean Sea. The accommodation was getting warmer as there was no air conditioning. I shared a cabin with another boy called Brian Morgan, a lad from Liverpool. My first night on board the lads, who were a lot older than me, gave me beer and I became drunk for the first time ever and had a terrible hangover the next morning. I had to be up at six to draw the stores for the pantry from the second steward. We had twelve first class passengers on board and they were well looked after. All good food and waited on by first class stewards. My job was to make all the salads, grind the coffee beans by hand and wash all the dishes.

The heat was starting to get to me as we were nearing the Suez Canal. At night to cool the cabin we used to stick these big tin things out of the port hole and which would help the air come in the cabin. We also had blowers.

The chief cook was from South Wales. His name was Taffy Sheppard. He seemed to take delight in giving me a hard time. I think he liked a drink. The rest of the crew were ok. Just over a week later we arrived at Port Said, Egypt ready to transit the Suez Canal. It was a lovely sunny morning and the ship was boarded by numerous people of all trades – barbers, shop keepers etc. – the bum boat man they call it – and the gilly gilly man, who used to do magic tricks with chicks and also clean you out if you weren't careful. You had to keep your cabin locked at all times and the port holes closed as they were renowned thieves. Most of the stuff they sold was junk – camels stuffed with sand, photo albums and Egyptian stuff. I did buy some of it but was told it was rubbish.

The barber could speak any dialect and while he was cutting my hair he was talking away to me in a Liverpool accent. Once he had finished I told the lads the barber was from Liverpool. They just laughed and told me he was Egyptian – apparently he learnt it all from when the British Army stationed there. It was funny to listen to him.

We went through the Suez Canal that night coming out the next morning to discover we were in the Red Sea, destination Aden (a British protectorate at the time). Three days down the Red Sea we then arrived in Aden where we docked for a few hours to refuel. The bum boats came out. Their stuff was better quality than in the Suez. Radios and cameras, more of them and cheaper than you would buy at home. My wage now was £16 a month, with overtime it was £20 – a big deal. Don't forget I was on £12 a week on the *Buffalo*, sometimes more with holidays. I did join the Seaman's Union in 1962 – you had to be in it to get a job, and besides it was the union that fought for your rises.

After Aden we proceeded to Penang, a small Malaysian island about a week from Aden, arriving again on a Sunday morning, by which time the weather was really hot. Crossing the Indian Ocean was really nice. We had bingo nights with the passengers and the officers in the saloon. I wasn't too keen on it but went along. The captain I remember was very strict. We had inspection every day and he hardly said a word to you. He was old-fashioned I suppose, not like captain Miller on the *Buffalo*. He had also been to deep sea with the *Thomas Brocklebank Company* who used to run out to India and the Red Sea ports.

Some of the passengers got off here at Penang, as a lot of them worked there in government jobs. As the British had to hand back to the Malays, these people were a mixture of all nationalities – Malay, Indonesian, Indian and Chinese. They get on well and I found them to be a lovely race of people.

The next port of call was to be Port Swettenham (Port Klang it is now), only a small port in a river surrounded by jungle. While I was there I went to the Seaman's Club where they had a swimming pool. It's only a day's run from Penang.

Following Port Swettenham we went to Singapore, the main discharge port. We used to go to a bar there called Tobies Paradise which was frequented by all the seamen… and plenty of local girls. The weather was really hot now. It was also a good place to buy things like stereo equipment, radios, cameras, suits – you name it they had it.

After discharging we then proceeded to Hong Kong where almost all of the passengers disembarked. We spent about a week there discharging cargo into the Chinese junks out in the harbour. It was truly a lovely view. Wally the second steward took me up to the peak tram to visit friends of his, which was a nice experience. You could also get suits made. The tailors would come out on a launch and measure you up. We would pay for the suits then and pay on our homeward bound journey from Japan.

After discharge we then went up to mainland China, Shanghai and Sinkiang. It was communist run at the time, and on arrival we were boarded by all kinds of military personnel, so we were restricted as to where we could go – just a visit up town and back. We had Chinese crew firemen who worked in the engine room. They were always nervous of the communists in case they were taken off the ship, but most of them were Hong Kong Chinese. It was an interesting place though.

We then left for Kobe in Japan, a place I really liked – especially the girls there! There used to be a place called Motamachi which was full of bars and shops. Japan was expensive but I bought a 52-piece dinner set for my mother which I still have today. It cost about £5 but it is really nice. I also bought a coffee set.

Most nights I was up at the bar with all the girls. There were some beautiful women there. Japan was always my favourite country. We would do about four or five ports – Nagoya, Shimazu, Yokohama, Otaru and Nagasaki, and then we would start to load cargo for the homeward-bound run to the UK calling back at Hong Kong, Singapore, Port Swettenham and Penang loading palm oil, rubber… you name it. After leaving Penang we went to Colombo, Ceylon (now called Sri Lanka), a small island off India. Whilst there I had a half day and went up to visit Kandy, the temple of the tooth, a fascinating place. After loading tea we set sail for Aden for 'bunkers' fuel then on down to the Red Sea eventually arriving at Suez . By this time everyone had the 'channels', which meant we were all happy due to the fact we would be home in just over a week. After leaving the Suez Canal we went on through the Mediterranean Sea until we passed Gibraltar. It was December so all the blue sky and sea had gone.

Going through the Bay of Biscay was rough seas. We eventually arrived in Liverpool on 7th December on a cold and frosty morning. The ship was spotless as the deck crew had painted all the ship. They were always clean when we arrived home. The full ship's compliment then was about 60 crew and twelve passengers. I could not wait to get home to see my parents and give my mother her tea set.

When I arrived home to the house I lived in in Belle Vale, my family had moved to a new house in Halewood, as my dad had taken a new job as a lorry driver in *Ford's* factory, so I got a taxi there. I used to leave my mother £5 a week out of my wages and still give her a few bob when I got home. I enjoyed giving her the money.

That was the end of my first deep sea trip out to the Far East. In January I would be going back on the same ship back out to the Far East. I was to spend two years on the ship and made a lot of friends. One of them I am still friends with to this day, Alby Brown. I was to meet him on my next trip – it was to be his first trip to sea, so I had two years ahead of him. Alby only went away to sea for a few years, until 1966 I think. He got married to a girl named Kathleen and had a son and daughter. I was having too much of a good time with the girls in the Far East. As soon as I had a few bob I was away up the road.

My favourite place was always Japan. A 16-year-old lad could not go wrong there! One place in Japan I did remember well was Nagasaki. I went to the museum where it showed pictures of the after effects of the atomic bomb dropped on the city in the Second World War.

After my time on the *Menestheus* I was to do one more trip with *Blue Funnel Line* which was on the *Perseus*, a bigger vessel than *Menestheus* and carried about 24 passengers. I liked that ship better. I did get to see many different countries whilst there and I wanted to move on elsewhere.

I thought I would try the Norwegian ships as there was an office in Liverpool, in Harrington Street, so I went there and applied for a job. I was accepted and soon I joined my ship. It was a Swedish ship called *M/S Norma*, belonging to a company called *Transmarine* of Halsingborg, Sweden. I was to spend one year on it trading between UK, Baltic Ports, Sweden, Denmark, North Africa and Spain. I sailed with many nationalities and I soon learned the Swedish language after a year. I also joined the Swedish Seaman's Union. Then I paid off the ship in Halsingborg after German and British seamen asked me to go to Germany with them on another ship. So I tossed a coin – should I go or stay in Sweden? Take another Swedish ship? After all, I had learned the language well enough to get by for a 17-year-old. Anyway I tossed up the coin and I stayed in Sweden. I then made my way up to Gothenburg to find another ship. It was January and it was freezing cold as you can imagine. I stayed in Halsingborg for a night and took the train to Gothenburg the next day.

I reported in for a job shortly after that, but the only job they had for me was a British tanker called the *Beechwood*. I wanted to go back on the Swedish ships but money was short, so I took the job as a galley boy. The company the ship belonged to was called *John Isaac Jacobs*. It had about ten ships – I think they went worldwide.

I joined the ship that evening in Gothenburg. Most of the crew were from Belfast. The next morning we were on our way to the Persian Gulf to load oil in Iraq for the UK. Funnily enough the ship went back to Belfast with the cargo after about six weeks, so I signed back on. I met the new crowd that joined and a few days later we got orders to sail to Beaumont, Texas USA, to load grain for Bombay, India. It took us 15 days across to the Mexican Gulf.

It was 1966 and the Beatles were riding high in the music charts and were very popular worldwide. It was the time of the hippies and top American bands such as the Birds and Jimi Hendrix, as well as a lot of British bands like The Rolling Stones and The Who.

Actually before we went to Beaumont we laid up in a small town called Port Neches whilst waiting to load our consignments of grain for India. After crossing the Atlantic from Belfast we had to clean and prepare the tanks for the grain cargo. So we all had to go down into the tanks at sea and clean them, a dirty job. They were then buttworthed with cleaning liquid that got rid of the traces of crude oil. At the end of the day we got a tot of four *Bells* rum – you were only allowed six cans a day then.

Port Neches was a lovely little town. We were not allowed to drink alcohol as you had to be over 18, but we made a lot of friends there and they took us over the state line where it was easy to get hold of beer. We spent three weeks there and it was one of the best times I have had. Meeting people and getting taken back to their homes for dinner. We went to mass on Sunday and the priest gave us all dinner. It was around Easter time and the weather was lovely. The lads off the ship where great. They were all from Belfast, both Catholics and Protestants who nevertheless all mixed well together. The troubles had not come to the province yet.

As usual all good things come to an end and we finally left Texas. It was an evening and all the friends we had met flashed their lights as we sailed down the river to the Gulf of Mexico. We were never to meet again however. It was a sad day for all, but such is the way of a seaman's life. Another adventure awaited us thousands of miles away east of the Suez Canal.

We were fully loaded with grain and it was a slow ship so it took us 14-16 days to Port Said where we waited to transit the Suez Canal the next day. It takes a day to go from one end to the other, stopping in the bitter lakes to let the other convoy through then out into the Red Sea. Next stop Aden to bunker fuel, then onto Bombay where we were to be anchored for three months along with hundreds of other ships with the same cargo before we went alongside to discharge the grain. I enjoyed my time in Bombay even though we were at anchor for many weeks, as there were so many ships awaiting discharge. We could still get ashore by launch, and I found the Indian people so friendly even though there was a lot of poverty which was very sad... but so many things to do. I remember the railway station built in Victorian times and old steam trains that travelled many miles across the sub-continent. After weeks at anchor we finally went alongside which was better for us as we could go ashore every night. I have never seen so many rats running up and down the quay! A lot of the dock workers just slept alongside the sheds with the rats going past them – they were used to it I suppose.

After a few weeks alongside we sailed out of Bombay to await orders for where we were to go next. We then proceeded to the Persian Gulf to load crude oil at Mina Ala Mhadi. It took us over a week to get there and we went alongside and loaded in over 24 hours. We got orders to sail for Hamburg to discharge, then after that to Newcastle where we all got off as the ship was dry-docking.

Everyone was happy too, as they had been away from home for seven months. I myself was away for over twelve months as I was on the Swedish ship before the *Beechwood*, and I was looking forward to going home. Going back to Europe was nice weather as it was summer time then. We came out of the Persian Gulf and into the Red Sea, through Suez and into the Mediterranean Sea passing Gibraltar on the starboard side and Morocco on the port side. A lovely sight, deep blue sea and light blue sky. What more can anyone ask for? This was the life. I just loved life at sea. After all I was 18 years of age now and hopefully had many more years ahead.

We soon arrived in Hamburg spending three days there, during which we sampled the delights of the city. The night life was great. It was 1966 and lots of different bands from the UK and USA were playing the nightclubs. From there it was over to Newcastle where we were we paid off. It was a Saturday when we caught the train down to Liverpool. As a lot of the lads were from Belfast they had to catch the ferry on Saturday night. We got to Liverpool around five o'clock at night. I took the lads to the Bears Paw pub in Liverpool where we celebrated our pay off. It was a great atmosphere. As I said, one of the best and happiest times of my career at sea was with these lads from Belfast, and I will never forget it. They went home that night and so did I – to see my family after twelve months away was nice.

The first thing I did was box my mother off with money, even though I left her an allotment every week. That was the thing to do in those days. I was not married but I lived at home. They were happy to see me and after visiting friends and family I decided to go over to Belfast and ship out from there, looking up my friends from the last ship. I went over on the ferry from Liverpool and arrived at a mate's place. His name was Jimmy O'Neill and had been with me on the *Beechwood*. Jimmy was married with two young children and he kindly let me stay with them for the few weeks I was there. He lived in the Falls Road area of Belfast (which was predominately Catholic), in a two bedroom terraced house in Sultan Street. The 'Troubles' had not yet started but as an outsider I could sense something brewing. My friend wanted to come ashore to work as he did not want to continue at sea, which was understandable really. Although as a Catholic it was difficult for him to find work. I visited friends on both sides but the Catholics seemed to get the rough end of the stick. The lads on the other side treated me just the same. We would all meet up together in the town centre and sometimes we would go up to the Shankill Road to visit them – great people.

There was no work for me over there so I came back to Liverpool. I always remember Jimmy O'Neill asked me to inform people at home of exactly what life was like for the Catholics in Belfast at that time. The trouble was about to start. Once I'd explained the situation to my mother, we were both sympathetic to them, especially as we were from Catholic backgrounds too. Although we had never experienced such problems, I do believe it was a bit sectarian in Liverpool a long time ago – but not the same as over there. When the Troubles did start many friends came over to visit me from Belfast. They were on a ship in Liverpool and were both Catholic and Protestant lads. My mother was a little worried by all these lads coming to our house, but she nevertheless treated them well.

I was to stay at home for about seven months because the pool doctor would not pass me fit for sea owing to my partial blindness. I was really disappointed, but I did get a medical with *Cunard Line* and they took me on as a mess man on the cargo ship *Samaria* going to New York. I did two trips before getting involved in a dispute on the ship and got finished up. However, I went back to the pool and eventually passed my medical eyesight test. The reason was they let me use my own hands to cover my eyes, which goes to prove where there is a will there is a way. Incidentally, when the 1966 seamen's strike broke out, we had already sailed from the UK on the *Beechwood*. We did want to go on strike in the USA at the time but as striking abroad was forbidden and doing so would have resulted in a prison sentence we didn't. When I first went to sea I was a union member – I even joining the Swedish Seamen's Union for the time I was there. I still have the union book to this day. I re-joined the National Union of Seamen when I joined the *Beechwood* and I am still a member. Today it is called the Rail, Maritime and Transport Union.

My next vessel was a ship called the *Ronsard* which belonged to a company from Liverpool called *Lamport and Holt*. It ran a service to Brazil, Argentina and Uruguay in South America. That was in 1967 and I did one trip on that ship. I enjoyed it but never had any money which was down to all the women in those lovely ports in South America! I was away three-and-a-half months. South America was a lovely place – Buenos Aires, Montevideo, Santos and Rio de Janeiro. I was to visit them again later in my life. The crew was a good one, mostly from Liverpool.

After a few weeks home I got a job on a *Shell* tanker called the *Hinea*, an 'H' class boat. We sailed around the UK coast and then we got orders to go to the Caribbean Islands, mostly running between the Maracaibo Lakes, Venezuela, Curacao, Aruba and the islands to the east coast of the USA. It was not one of my best trips and I was glad to pay off that. Funnily enough, I paid off in Newcastle after four-and-a-half months.

The following year in 1968, my next vessel which belonged to *Harrison* was a heavy lift ship with a big Stulkan capable of lifting 200 tonne. She went to South Africa, Thomas and Jos Harrison Line, Cape Town, Walvus Bay, East Coast, Port Elizabeth, Durban, Lourenco Marques and Beira East Africa. From there I came home and joined a ship called the *Swan River* belonging to *Houlder Brothers*. She was a kind of tramp ship and went to wherever she got a charter. On tramp ships you can get some really good ports and countries, which was what I liked about them. You just did not know where you would end up. Funnily enough we went to South Africa on a *Clan Line* charter and then went to load sugar for a sugar line charter in Port Louise, Mauritius. I liked it there too, striking up a friendship with an able seaman by the name of Mick Kirkby. Mick was also from Liverpool and had been on the *Adventurer* with me and a steward called Rudy Gellano from Trinidad. I still see Rudy today in town. He hasn't changed much, just a little bit older. I never saw Mick Kirkby again.

The apartheid problem in South Africa at the time never bothered me or Rudy. We would just bring the women on board. That was a good trip. A lot of the lads you sailed with you never saw again for a long time, if ever. They call it board of trade acquaintance. I wanted to go back in to the galley properly as a cook, so after that trip I went to catering college in Liverpool for a three week course to get a second cook and baker's certificate. I really enjoyed the school and made a lot of friends. I learnt basic cooking and bread and cake making, which incidentally I enjoyed doing more. Looking back now I wish I had gone on to be a full-time baker working on the cruise ships. But I got to go to more interesting places on cargo ships and other vessels. On board ship I was baking a lot of bread, cakes and pastries etc. and also working alongside experienced bakers and cooks. I've picked up a great deal of knowledge. I was enjoying my life – it was the swinging sixties after all!

Every afternoon we would go over to a pub called the Eagle which was across from the catering college for a few pints. We would often continue in to the night, turning up the next morning with big hangovers. How we got through it I don't know. But we had some of the best teachers in the country, with many of them from the old Cunard Liners – *Queen Elizabeth*, *Queen Mary* and *Empress b*oats – you name it. They were all time served chefs and bakers. The younger teachers were also very good and would sometimes accompany us across to the pub at lunchtime. Often there was Billy Byrnes, a chef-teacher. His fellow teachers used to joke that if he couldn't be found anywhere, just go to the Eagle where he'd be having a pint with his class! But you could never fault him (I mention him later). He knew his stuff did Billy Byrnes.

After passing out, we went back to the pool Shipping Federation where the lads used their contacts to get us our next jobs. I was to make my first trip as second cook and baker. I reported to the 'Shipping Federation' – or 'The Pool' as it was known – and I was offered a job as assistant cook which I took on a ship called the *Arcadian*. It was not a very old ship. It belonged to another big Liverpool shipping company called *Ellerman Papayanni*. They owned numerous ships – *Ellerman Hall Line*, *Ellerman*, *Bucknall* and so on. They went out to the Persian Gulf, India and Pakistan, the occasional charter world wide. The *Ellerman Papayanni* just went to the nearby ports such as Cyprus, Egypt and Israel for fruit, as well as Portugal. They were known as the market boats by the seamen, usually doing four to six week trips. I think at one time four *Papayanni* ships were chartered in Borneo. The *Ellerman Hall Line* ships were all named after cities. Stricks were named after places in Northern Pakistan.

It was just before Christmas when we sailed for Ashdod, Israel, to load citrus fruit before returning to Cardiff where I paid off after a four week trip. After a few weeks home I reported to the Shipping Federation.

Chapter 3
Shanghaied

Iwas called to join a ship from the *Blue Star Line* called the *Newcastle Star*, named after the port in Australia where the ship traded a lot. I joined her in Liverpool only to take it to London bound for New Zealand and Australia. I was only on it for two weeks. I did not fare too badly on my first trip as second cook – I excelled more in my baking but it was to give me good experience for the future. I enjoyed the stay in London where I also managed to see Liverpool play West Ham. I then went home and waited for another job. My next job was on a *Shaw Saville* ship called the *Doric*. Once again I joined in Liverpool and was on it for around two weeks sailing around the coast. It was an old ship but it had steam ovens which were great for baking bread. Even today those ovens take some beating – they just don't make them like that anymore. I left the ship in Southampton and got a job on the *Northern Star* one of the passenger ships belonging to *Shaw Saville*. We went around the world – Las Palmas, South Africa, Australia, New Zealand, Tahiti, Mexico, Panama Canal, Caribbean, Curacao, Trinidad, Barbados and Jamaica – then home. It was a three month trip and my job on there was one of three vegetable cooks. It was too hot for me – besides I preferred to be on the cargo ships – but it was nevertheless an experience for me. I came home from Southampton and a few weeks later I joined another *Shaw Saville* ship called the *Persic*, which was another old ship but I enjoyed it. It had the same old galley and ovens. I was only coasting on it for a few weeks, but the regular run this ship did was to Australia and New Zealand, usually for three to four months at a time.

Liverpool was really jumping with the music and pub scene, with groups playing in the afternoon in clubs and the pubs were great.

The pubs most seamen frequented then were the Trawler and the Red Lion across from the shipping federation on Mann Island. Then the Queens or the Monas, as it was known then. The Pen and Wig was a popular pub next to the Crocodile in Harrington Street. You went downstairs to it. I always remember Hetty and Barbara, two sisters who worked there. They were really good to us seamen, lending us money or a 'sub' as it was called. If we were short then we would pay them back at a later date. Most of the lads I knew drank there, and lads off the *Empress of Canada* went there all dressed in their smart clothes, KD trousers and combo shoes stitched at the sides. You could always tell a seaman. Just across the road was a pub called Why Not. A couple called Elsie and Les ran it and it was a favourite haunt of the *Harrison Line* boys as well as the lads off the *Norwegian Pool* above.

The next job I had was on the *Colorado Star*, a *Blue Star* vessel. I joined in Liverpool then went up to Glasgow to load whisky and general cargo for the West Coat of the USA, going through Panama calling at Los Angeles, San Francisco, Oakland, Seattle and Vancouver, then back down again and home to London. I enjoyed it on there – it was a good run away for three months. When my leave was up I went to the pool where they gave me a job on the *Lamport and Holt* ship *Roland*. It used to be called the *Dunedin Star*. It was quite an old ship and would be my second *Lamport and Holt* ship. I went down to sign on and coming off the ship were a few seamen I knew. Eddie Devlin was one and he managed to tell me beforehand to make sure I got on it, as it was only away for two months to Brazil and back. I went on board and looked around the galley, introduced myself to the cook Bob Ng, who was of English Chinese and originally from Liverpool. He was about my own age. I was to be the second cook. I noticed that there was no bread machine except a big bread bin. I was told I had to make bread by hand. I did not fancy that as well as pastries. Still, I could put up with it for two months. It was October 1969 and I signed on. I thought I would be home for Christmas – little did I know what surprise lay ahead.

We finally sailed from Liverpool to Las Palmas for bunkers (engine fuel). It was an old steam ship if I remember. Anyway, just before we arrived there the captain received a telegram from the Liverpool office to say that the ship would be going on charter to a Brazilian company and that we would be away a few months longer. When we heard which ports we'd be going to, I did not mind at all because I was single, although a lot of the married seamen weren't happy. The run we were going on included Brazilian ports, Buenos Aires, Montevideo, Cape Town, Durban, East Africa then across to Singapore, Penang, Malaysia, Hong Kong, Kobe, Nagoya, Yokohama plus a few other ports in Japan, then back again to load for East Africa, Lorenzo Marques, Beira, Durban, Cape Town, Brazil and Argentina, then back up to Brazil, finish loading the cargo for Europe and back to Liverpool July 1970.

I enjoyed the trip even though it was hard work doing the bread by hand, especially if I had been on the ale the night before! On our last leg of the voyage between Brazil and Argentina, two other lads and I went ashore in Santos (which was a lovely place) for a few drinks. We were enjoying ourselves when suddenly we heard the ships funnel blowing for departure, so we decided to drink up and get a move on. Just as we got to the quay the lads were letting go to sail and the gangway was still down so we ran to try and get aboard. The old man decided to bring up the gangway. We could easily have made it but they sailed without us. What could we do? We went back to the bar and had a few more drinks before going to see the agent to find out what the situation was. After all, the ship was only going to the next port which was not that far away. It was decided that we would be re-joining the ship in Buenos Aires and they would fly us down in a week's time. We stayed in Santos for the week, mainly being fussed over and looked after by the girls in the bars.

When we finally did re-join the vessel we had to pay for the air fare of the two Brazilian police officers who escorted us to Argentina, as well as our own air fare which was a lot of money then. When we arrived on board the captain was mad, saying he was going to log us as well. I spoke to the two other ship mates, a lad from Warrington and one from South Wales. My stance was to refuse to work if this was his position, as it had already cost me near enough all of my remaining wages. It was therefore not worth my while working. The CH/steward came down and said if you all turn for work the captain will not log you and not give you a bad report. So we said ok, but when we got home he gave us a bad discharge or DR we called it (decline to report), plus the fact that we had no money left when we arrived in Liverpool. The air fares alone were £400, which was a lot of money then. I remember I docked on the Sunday afternoon in Liverpool after nine months away and had to go to the pool for a disciplinary hearing before shipping out again the following Friday on the *Empress of Canada*. Mind you, that was a good trip. Apart from that episode the old man reneged on his promise to us.

I do recall steaming in to Durban, South Africa, where we saw a *Harrison Line* ship which called there regularly. As we were passing their ship the lads were asking us if we were lost, as the *Lamport and Holt* ships didn't normally go to Durban. We also had a few lads pay off in Buenos Aires due to illness. Two lads, one named King and the other Queen, were in beds next to each other in hospital. How about that? King and Queen! I went down to the *Canadian Pacific* office at the pier head where they offered me a new job as an assistant baker, so I went down to the ship which was berthed at the landing stage in Liverpool where all the passenger ships went. I reported to the CH/Baker and he said the ship was sailing the next day so start work at 6am, which I did. We went across to Montreal, Canada and back. I loved working in the bake house with the two bakers. I picked up a lot for the short time I was there, from both the baker and the confectioners. The baker's name was Joe Mottram, from Scotland Road. He grew up with my mother's family. There was another bloke, Arthur Morris, a real character. Both were nice men to work with. Joe was CH/baker on nights and Arthur was second baker on days with me. They certainly knew their jobs, as well as the confectioners Hugh Daws and Peter Brown. However, I was to do only one trip in the bake house as the lad who was permanent came back. They offered me a job in the still room in charge of coffee and tea and making the catering staff tea and toast of a morning, along with various other jobs. I would sit in the cinema of an afternoon – the lads paid me 50p at the end of the trip so I made a lot of money there.

Even though I enjoyed my jobs I was itching to get back to the faraway places. I was not yet ready to settle in one company as some of the lads, did but I wonder what would have happened if I had got a permanent job in the bake house? I would probably still be there. They were a good crowd of lads and, thanks to the quality of the chefs, served excellent food.

After my time on *The Empress* I was sent over to Birkenhead Docks to join an iron ore carrier belonging to a company called *Silver Line* as second cook. We went to a place in North West Africa called Nouadhibou Mauritania where we loaded iron ore for Newport, South Wales. I was only away for a couple of weeks, but it wasn't a bad trip. The next week I would go down to the pool and see what was going on job wise before going to the Pen and Wig to meet up with the lads and stay until 3.00pm. That was the closing time then, but you could always get a drink at 3pm in the clubs. Yankee Clipper was one of them. It was open until 6pm. We would come out of there then go back to the pub until 11pm before ending up in the *She Club*. When I look back I don't know how I did it, day in day out! Mind you, I would rest up on Saturday and Sundays.

The Yankee Clipper was run by Sonny Philips and his wife, Theresa, who were always very good to us, probably because between the hours of three and six their best customers were dockers and seamen. There was always good music, plenty of drink and good friends. The other clubs were the Ranleigh and Curzon. Mind you, there were a lot of clubs you could go to then.

The next Monday morning I would report to the pool. Geoff Fryer was one of the people who gave out the jobs. "Got a good job for you there Eddie," he said. "What's that then?" I replied. It was an iron ore ship going to West Africa for four weeks. They needed a second cook. I decided to take it as there was nothing much doing. I joined the ship called *Rivelaux* in Birkenhead which belonged to the *Bolton Steam Ship*, my namesake. I signed on and the old man jokingly asked me if I was related to the company owners.

Anyway, we sailed to Port Etienne, West Africa and loaded iron ore for South Wales. I only did one trip there. Then I was sent over to join the sister ship called the *Ribble Head* iron ore ship but was only on it a day in Birkenhead dry dock before getting another job on a tanker belonging to a company called *Turnball and Scott*. It was a tramp ship company which meant you could go anywhere in the world. The name of the tanker was the *East Gate*. I joined it over in Stanlow Oil Refinery by Manchester Ship Canal. It had just arrived from Seattle, USA. I thought this would do me, looking forward to going somewhere nice, but I was only on there for four weeks. All we were doing was trading around the UK and the continent. It was winter time and as there was no sign of going to the tropics I paid off in Stanlow on 17th December.

The lads were from all over the UK. The chief cook was a fella called Charlie McLennan, a big man from the south end of Liverpool. Charlie was a character who loved his drink. I would be up at six in the morning to start breakfast but there would be no sign of Charlie until 9am. The first thing he would say to me was, "Sorry Ed, the petrol fumes outside my port hole are knocking me out." I just used to laugh. It was the alcohol fumes more like! He would keep late hours every night drinking with the pump man who was a big giant of a man from Bristol called Tiny. Charlie was an excellent cook and baker. He had worked for some of the best companies and I learned a lot from him in those few weeks. I used to see him from time to time before he passed away some years ago. I went to school with his brother Tommy who I think is on the Australian coast now. Charlie treated me ok – I liked him and he was funny to work with.

When I went back to the pool, Geoff Fryer said he had another good job for me again. Mind you, there used to be a big noticeboard on the wall and all the names of the ships would be up there with whatever rating they needed. Rating is the job title e.g. stewards, cooks, firemen, greasers etc. You knew where most of the ships were going to, most of them on regular runs. A lot were Liverpool companies, *P.S.N.C.*, *Ellerman*, *Moss Hutchinson* and *Federal Line*. You could practically pick where you wanted to go then. With the exception of the tramp ships, you could pick anywhere in the world. North East companies like *Chapman and Willan*, *Alan Blacks* of Newcastle or somewhere near there – the baron boats. If you fancied a long trip you could jump on one of them as you were guaranteed to be away for a long time. You could see the world. What a life! As a result of the demise of the merchant navy and the decreasing number of companies, you just can't do that today.

There were always coastal jobs to be had as well as passenger ferries with plenty of work on them. Don't forget, you had the shipping federation all in the big sea ports around the UK. You could end up sailing with Geordies from Newcastle, Taffs from Wales, Jocks from Scotland and Irish lads from Southern and Northern Ireland. A good mixed crowd – I don't think I have been with a bad lot really.

Anyway back to Geoff Fryer. I was a second cook/baker on a *Shaw Saville* boat called *Ceramic* which was going to Australia and New Zealand for four months. So I jumped at the opportunity and went down and signed on. You could get an advance note then and chance it in town. Like a sub it was. I had a look around the galley. It was a big ship, 12,000 ton, as it had previously carried 100 passengers, although not now. There was a chief cook, second cook and baker (myself), assistant cook, galley boy, six stewards, chief steward and second steward. I think a crew of 60 or more. I remember they had a lot of engine room staff besides the engineers. I found a lot of these men very interesting to talk to when amongst them socialising. The older ones especially had been on coal burners shovelling coal on the old steam ships. A lot had been torpedoed during the war, many numerous times. They were hardened men of all sizes. Very funny the tales they would tell you. One instance stood out when we sailed on the *Ceramic* weeks later, arriving at the Port of New Plymouth with Mount Taranaki in the background. It was a beautiful place. We were to load butter and cheese for the UK.

Anyway back to my story. There was one fireman out on the deck having a beer. We did have a bar on there, more of which later. However, there was a Japanese ship in loading timber. The crew were all looking over to us. They were wearing helmets for safety on deck and a kind of military uniform. From a distance you would think they were soldiers. Poor Jimmy the fireman had started to get a bit drunk and was shouting over to them, "Tojo's dead, the war is over." It was quite hilarious when I look back. The Japanese thought Jimmy was waving at them. After a while Jimmy sat down and started to nod off, then along came his mate Tommy McNally, another character, and started talking in Japanese and wearing a straw Japanese hat standing over poor Jimmy saying, "English soldier bow to Japanese officer now or today, tomorrow you die." Poor Jimmy got back up and he didn't know where he was and started shouting back at Tommy, "Tojo's dead the war's over." Then he turned to the Japanese and continued shouting at them. I've no idea what they thought was happening but it was hilarious. Jimmy was a lovely man who had two sons at sea – Mick, who was with us that trip, and another son also on deck. There were a lot of characters on that trip. I have never laughed so much.

We sailed non-stop from Liverpool on the *Ceramic*, via Cape Town. Our first port was Fremantle, Australia, a lovely place. As I said before, it had a bar on board which had previously belonged to the passengers when they carried them, but the crew managed to get it. It was really big with a huge lounge with arm chairs. Two of the stewards ran the bar, one named Dominic and the other Thelma. Yes, they were 'queens' as we called them at sea. They were a good laugh and very witty, but once on the Aussie coast and New Zealand a lot of people would come on board from ashore as the bar never closed. There was plenty of drink and women. Dominic would dress up as a woman. Sometimes I would think she did better than us for copping off. Mind you, I think the fellas she had picked up, who were obviously worse for wear at the time, would get a shock when they woke up with her the next morning! We all had single berth accommodation mind you, that was really good. On the way out in the tropics, the lads rigged up a swimming pool made out of canvas and timber and at night they would show the old Walport films reel to reel on deck using a white sheet as the screen. It was the highlight of the trip. We always looked forward to it. We changed them three or four times during the trip. My mates Tony Rice, Sid Malone, Jo Stone, Tony Summers and Phil Unsworth were on there with me.

After Fremantle we went to Melbourne, Adelaide, Sydney and Brisbane – all were very nice especially Brisbane. We went to a place called Breakfast Creek on the river. We loaded lamb there, general cargo outward bound and refrigerated on the way home. Brisbane is lovely but very hot. Then we went across to New Zealand, Auckland and New Plymouth. After loading there we set off for Panama transiting through the canal and calling at Curacao to take on fuel. Unfortunately we had to pay the bosun off with a heart attack. His name was John Tully, a big man. We then continued across the Atlantic to our home port, from where we had started out. It had taken us four months around the world to the same dock we had left four months before. We all paid off and met up in the Monas pub in Town.

That was the best when you paid off – a few bob in your pocket and met up with your family and friends. Funny, really, having just spent four months with the same lads you would meet up with them when you pay off. That was the way it was then – good camaraderie, everyone knew you were a seaman because you could tell them a mile away. I still see a few of the lads off that ship to this day. Sid Malone, one of my mates, passed away a few years ago leaving a wife and kids. I dare say a lot more of the crew, especially the old firemen, are no longer with us. After all it was 37 years ago. 1971.

I had never sailed on ferry boats so I tried one in the summer of 1971. It was on a ship called the *Cambria* belonging to *British Rail*. The regular run for that particular one was between Holyhead and Ireland, but as the bridge connecting the Menai Strait caught fire they moved up to Heysham. You did a week on and a week off. The money you made was really good, far more than you got deep sea. It was a better agreement – no wonder the lads stayed on them. It was ideal for the married blokes. I did two weeks on there as I was itching to get back to deep sea. John Fitzgerald was on there with me and Terry Duffy – they were good lads and a good laugh.

It was getting near Christmas and I got a job on the *Canadian Star*, another *Blue Star* ship. I worked by for a week then sailed around Europe, Scandinavia, Sweden and Denmark. I met a girl in Denmark in a place called Aahrus. Anyway, we wrote to each other for a while but nothing came of it. We got back to Liverpool and the ship changed its name to the *Raeburn*, one of the *Lamport Holt Line*. I did not know at the time that *Blue Star*, *Lamport Holt* and *Booth Line* were all one company. We sailed to Brazil, Montevideo and Uruguay and Las Palmas on the way down. It was a three month trip in total. The chief cook was Mark Wong, just a few years older than me, who also came from Liverpool. I still see him today. He had to pack in the sea due to ill health. It was a good trip as always on that run, plenty of laughs and plenty of women. Also, we were away for three-and-a-half months and came back to discharge cargo at Avonmouth and Liverpool. I only did the one trip there.

I was home for a little while when I decided to call the *Blue Star Line* to see if they had work for me. At that time the head office was in London. Two days later, to my surprise, I was sent to join a new container ship called the *Columbia Star* in Liverpool. At first it seemed quite big and long, painted light grey over the hull with white accommodation and a big blue star funnel which you could see miles away. The *Blue Star* was renowned for that. I got on board and reported to sign on and see the chief cook. The accommodation at the time was out of this world – single berth cabins, en suite bathrooms and air conditioning. It was a truly modern vessel. The galley and mess rooms were very modern with first class ovens. It also has a bar in the recreation room. I went to see the cook, a lad from Liverpool, Dave Mac. I got on well with Dave as there was just us both in the galley along with Ginger the mess man from London, another character too. We went around Europe and Scandinavia discharging containers and loading them. We weren't in port long but we always managed to get ashore. The ship had a good speed of 20 knots. When we got back to Liverpool, Dave and Ginger got off as they were only relieving for the trip and another cook joined. I could not get on with him somehow, but I was there ten weeks counting the coastal run. The *Columbia Star* ran between Europe, Scandinavia and the west coast of the USA. The next trip I went on was its sister ship, the *California Star,* which was the very same. It was better on there. I then got another job on the *New Zealand Star.* It had a big heavy lift crane (200 tonne I think) and was a cargo ship built about 1967. I had to go down to London and stay in the Seaman's Mission as I was flying out to Cadiz, Spain, to join in the dry dock with the rest of the crew. We were there about four days before sailing for Napier, New Zealand via the Panama Canal.

The chief cook was only young – his name was Mick Barber, but know to everyone as Michelle. The mess man was from Cornwall or Devon called Dave. The two stewards were called Tom and Tony, aka Milly and Wendy! The second steward was a bit of a weirdo. He used to dress up in Khaki shirt, trousers immaculately pressed and tall black leather boots resembling someone out of the SS. His other name was Rose. What had I let myself in for? But to be honest it was an excellent trip full of laughs and adventure. The steward and cook were very witty being queens, and once we had reached Napier the fun would begin. It took us about four weeks to get to Napier, with good weather all the way down to New Zealand, and just a little bit of a bad storm leaving Cadiz.

Cadiz was a nice place. It was the first time I had been there. We stayed one night in the hotel when we first arrived and this AB seaman from New Zealand was drinking with us in the bar. He decided to go to bed, so he bade goodnight and asked me to call him in the morning as we would be going down to the ship. It was not long before I went. Anyway, I got up in the morning and called him. No answer, so I went down for breakfast and went back up to call him again. As there was still no sign of him, I told the steward Tony (Wendy). I told Tony I had called the lad twice and got no answer, so he went up to the room and found him dead. Apparently he had died of a heart attack. The police and doctor came and decided there was no foul play. A few days later we sailed and they boxed him up and put him on board. We had a short service two days out of Cadiz then put him over the side, the carpenter putting holes in the coffin so it would sink. After that we proceeded to our destination, first stop Panama Canal.

On the voyage down to Kiwi, as we called New Zealand, we called at Pitcairn Island which, as you know, was home to the descendent of Fletcher Christian and the rest of the seamen from the mutiny on the *Bounty*. We stopped for a few hours to take mail and give them flour and other stores. We would exchange the beautiful carvings they made. It was very interesting talking to them as they spoke with an old English accent from 200 years ago. They all had English names. I met an old man who they lifted from their long boat on to our ship. He must have been 80 years of age. That was 1972, so when I asked him what he was to Fletcher Christian, he told me he was his great-grandson. I had a camera and asked one of the other islanders who was related to Adams, another descendent of the mutineers, to take a photo, which he willingly did. Sadly, when I came to get it developed they never turned out. I was very disappointed as it's not every day you would get a picture of Fletcher Christian's grandson taken with you. I still think of that to this day. They go down to some island and bring their wood for the carvings. I bought a shark carved by one of the descendants of mutineer Jacob Warren. I still have it to this day. There is another island which is over-run with rats – so I was told by the second mate navigating officer. No one is allowed to go there. Apparently, a long time ago a sailing ship got wrecked there, and that's how they came to be there. Pitcairn Island is a beautiful sight to come upon. To the mutineers it was the ideal refuge from the Royal Navy sent out to fetch them back for trial. That's another story.

We eventually arrived in Napier on a beautiful December sunny morning. It was summer time in the Southern Hemisphere. Michelle, the chief cook, came up to me and the mess man just after lunch, telling us that a lot of shore-side people had come aboard to the crew bar. They were mostly women which was good. Soon the bar was jumping – just like a night club it was. Everywhere was closed in Napier on a Sunday with it being a small town, so everyone came down to the ship. We had plenty of beer and food. Michelle knew a lot of the girls as he had been there before. You know they got on well with the queens, so Michelle told us to look after them, which we did in more ways than one. We were in Napier for about 21 days, discharging and loading cargo, and it was one of the best times ever as far as women and partying went. All the crew had long hair like me. The top bands then, who the lads played in the ship's bar were Deep Purple, T Rex and Elton John. It was then that I first heard the Eagles' LP, 'Desperado'. Their music had not quite caught on in the UK as they were American, but as soon as I heard that LP I knew they would become a big band. That was 1972.

One Saturday night the mess man and I tried to have a night off the ale, so we took a couple of girls to the cinema and watched the Last Picture Show, which was a very good movie about a small time cinema. Just like the one we were in! After it finished, we went back to the ship and the bar was jumping. So another late night and hangover ensued. The local pub the lads would use was called the Cabana. That was great at night especially if you had a few ships in from the UK. Then we would all visit each other's ship. It was like a pub crawl. You had the *Port Line* ships, *Federal, Trinder, Andersons, Shaw Saville* line – you name it. You would sometimes be with those ships on the Kiwi and Australian coasts for weeks on end, getting to know all the crews in time. Some of the lads had their own band on the ship. The *Iberic* had a good band which used to play the old T Rex single, 'She lives on the coast and she's brighter than most...' – 'Hot Love', it was called. It became their theme song. They were good.

The crew we had on the *New Zealand Star* was mixed with Geordies, Highland Men, Londoners, Scousers, Irish and Welsh. We left Napier just before Christmas as we were all hoping to have Christmas in port, but no such luck. Once the cargo was completed we set sail. Everyone was sad to leave and not looking forward to being at sea again. As we went out of the bay we could see the *Adelaide Star*, another *Blue Star* ship, waiting to come alongside in our birth. They would definitely get to Christmas and New Year alongside the lucky buggers.

Going home was not too bad. Once we got the Christmas celebrations over everyone got back to their normal routine at sea. We in catering were kept very busy preparing Christmas dinner.

Christmas is always a busy time. Everyone enjoyed it. We had to make our own Christmas cakes and mince pies. Soon we would be arriving at the Panama Canal. I used to like going through it, it would take most of the day to get through from Bilbao to Cristobal and then into the Atlantic and Caribbean and homeward bound with a cargo of lamb. We docked in Southampton and paid off about 4 o'clock in the afternoon and then got the train home to Liverpool. It was the end of January 1973.

Chapter 4
Blue Star Line

I was to do five more trips on the *New Zealand Star*, mostly with the same crew running between Australia, New Zealand and the UK. We also stopped off at Pitcairn Islands where we gave the islanders store and bought carvings off them.

I left the *New Zealand Star* in 1974 after many good and happy trips. I was to be promoted to chief cook, so after a short spell of leave I was sent to the *Brasilia Star* to work in London for a few weeks. I never did a voyage on her. She was going to South America instead. I was to fly out and join the *Hobart Star* in Los Angeles USA. That ship was on what they called a crusader run trading between New Zealand, Fiji Islands, Hawaii, Honolulu, the West Coast of the USA and Canada. I joined In LA on 12th July. After a flight from London we loaded cargo up the coast to San Francisco, Portland, Oregon, Seattle, and Vancouver, then proceeded to Honolulu, then to Fiji Islands, and then New Zealand. The *Hobart Star* was a refrigerated cargo ship built about 1957, I think, and had seven hatches. We used to get about three to four weeks in New Zealand loading and discharging cargo up and down the coast. Our recreational room was down the other end of the ship but the lads turned it into a bar, which was like a little night club with all the strobe lighting. The main crew mess was mid-ship next to the galley and the PO mess was next to that. The cabins where small but nice. I had my own cabin. There was myself, a second cook, assistant cook, mess man, second steward and about four stewards. The whole crew totalled over 60. That was a very good ship and the lads would stay on there for a long time without coming home. Everyone wanted to go on that ship as it was a good party ship and very popular with the girls on the

New Zealand coast, plus the places it went to were good too. The crew on there where all mixed from all over the UK. Everyone had long hair then as all heavy metal bands were the thing – Deep Purple, Uriah Heap, Wishbone Ash, Pink Floyd – you name it the lads had the music. It was all cassette tape then, so we all used to bring out our own cassette recorders or buy them on the Fiji Islands as it was cheap there.

We spent Christmas 1974 in Suva – it was great there with plenty of beer on the ship and women. It had a lot of characters on it, especially amongst the old firemen who worked in the engine room. They would always come around my cabin for a drink as we had cold beer in the galley fridge. They would come up between watch keeping. Sometimes I was not going to bed until three in the morning and I was up at 6 o'clock. I came home off that ship 10 months later in April 1975. We flew home from Vancouver to London. There were two of us from Liverpool, me and an AB named Geoff Woodward from Marsh Lane, Bootle. He was a good lad who was on the ship at the same time. He is still about. I met his family but I've not seen Geoff since 1975 – I do believe he works in the offshore industry.

One thing I forgot to mention whilst the ship was in a port called Astoria up in Oregon on the west coast of USA, me and an AB John Sheldon from London found a nice little bar and were having great time with a good band playing plenty of beer and women. Astoria was a small town with very friendly people, and the scenery was truly wonderful with pine trees and mountains – just like being in a Western movie. Anyway, the lads on the ship phoned the bar we were in as they were with us early on and told us to get going as the ship was sailing. We thought it was a wind up as they were always doing that, and most of the time they were joking, but this time they weren't and we ended up in the local county jail for the night and day and then took a flight down to LA to join the ship. The captain was in a good mood as he was going home, so he let us off with a warning. Mick and Bruce Lee, the second cook and assistant cook coped ok whilst I was adrift and apart from a telling off from the chief steward all was ok.

When I look back they really were good times then. I wish you could turn the clocks back but there you go. I went home to see my family and I gave my mother some money to buy herself something. I was home for about four weeks and I was to join one of the new Reefer ships *Blue Star* had just had built. *The Afric Star* could carry fruit and meat and also general goods. We were to join it in Felixstowe, Suffolk. The ship had just come in from Cape Town on its maiden voyage. They were lovely ships built in Smith Dock, Middlesbrough in 1975. It was all single berth accommodation, modern with a big galley. Anyway, we travelled down on the midnight train to London then to Ipswich. We arrived on board the ship at around eight in the morning – five of us joined from Liverpool. These ships never had big crews in the galley just two of us – a second steward and two stewards, I think, and a boy rating – in total about thirty crew. We left Felixstowe and proceeded to Port Limon in Costa Rica. These ships were very fast, traveling at over twenty knots. We loaded bananas for Galveston, Texas, Boston and New York, then to Honduras, just running between those ports.

They were nice ships but not in port long. We spent the next four months on that run and then we came home from New York by aircraft to London. The ship was to stay out there for a few years. I was only home a few weeks and I found myself flying out to Vancouver to re-join *Hobart Star*. Sadly, I was only there two months when my mother died. The captain and the crew were very good. I was flown home from Auckland, New Zealand to Liverpool where I was met by my family. It was a sad time – she had died of a heart attack but I am glad that I was able to get home to bury her. She was a wonderful woman and I missed her a lot. When you think of it I never saw her a lot being away at sea so much, but I do remember something she said the morning I was to fly out to the *Hobart Star*. She said, "Don't forget to come home this Christmas," and I said, "Ok, since you asked me." Little did I know that would be the last time I would see her alive.

The lads had a collection – as they did when anyone had to go home. After the funeral my father and I wrote to them thanking everyone for their support. That was November 1975. There was only my dad and brother Jim living at home, as my two sisters were married by then. A few weeks later my boss telephoned me and asked me to go to Middlesbrough and joined a ship called the *Avelona Star*, which was one of the reefer ships, sister to the *Africa Star*. It was 18th December when I got the train up there and myself and the second steward, Tony Gallagher, stayed in the hotel for a week, just going down to the ship every day getting the store rooms and fridges ready for sea. It was still in the ship yard. The rest of the crew joined before Christmas and we sailed 18th December. Going down the river the welders were still doing the decks and it was snowing heavy. We got around to Zeebrugge to bunker, take on fuel and then proceeded over to Costa Rica.

It was a bad crossing on Christmas Day, and really hard to try and cook the dinner, but we managed. After a week the weather got better and we all settled down and arrived in port Limon, Costa Rica where we loaded for gulf port Mississippi and the east coast of the USA. I had sailed with three of the catering department before – Millie, Wendy and Keyhole Kate, as well as the second cook, Chris Wheatley, who was with me on the *Hobart Star* in 1974. So it was a good trip. You had to do four month trips then, and as the ships stay out there you nearly always flew home from New York for crew change. Costa Rica and the Gulf Ports were very nice. I met a nice girl there but again nothing came of it. Her name was Virginia. We made a lot of friends – most of the crew were all good to sail with and a lot of laughs, especially with the queens Millie, Wendy and Keyhole.

I came home in April 1976. When I got home I went up to my mother's grave. It had been six months since she had died. I visited family and friends, and then a month later I was to fly out to New York and join the Ulster Star in New Jersey. I remember we all got on a bus in Liverpool and went to Manchester airport. We had a few lads from Hull in the crew and a few lads I knew from other ships. Paul Kelly was my second cook and a lad from Doncaster, Phil, was assistant cook on the *Hobart Star* with me in 1974. The mess man was Joe Kelly – we had a good catering staff. We were in Jersey for five days, then we sailed down to the Panama Canal with orders for New Zealand to load mutton for Odessa, Russia in the Black Sea. It took us about five weeks to get to New Zealand. The Ulster Star was built in the 1950s old cargo boat style. The cargo was general with some refrigerated goods. We took general cargo there and I think we had some cargo for Russia.

The weather the way down was beautiful. We even had BBQs. We finally arrived in Littleton and there were quite a few ships in — you always see someone you know all over the world that you have sailed with. There where some good pubs in Littleton. We had five weeks there loading cargo. Today with the modern container ships you will only be a day or less — how times change! You could not beat the old cargo ship. It had character and bigger crews, like a close knit community. When the new container ships came out it was a big change all round. (I will come to that in a later chapter.) I just loved being at sea for weeks plodding along at a slow speed — blue skies and sea are a great life, always looking forward to getting to port.

We had a lot of parties on the *Ulster Star* nearly every night. Sometimes me and Paul, the second cook, would come out about 4am from the bar, get a shower and start work getting breakfast ready, then lunch and dinner. When I look back now I often think how I did that, but I was a lot younger then. Even the captain came to the galley one morning and said, "I don't know how you do it," but he was good as long as the job got done as then he didn't mind. We used to spend a lot of time in the British, a pub just outside the gate. All the seamen went there. We were often there afternoon and night. Littleton is a lovely place surrounded by big mountains, and as you got into port it is a beautiful site. It is on the South Island, not far from Canterbury. We were soon to leave. As we were loaded with mutton we sailed from New Zealand across the Tasman Sea and Australian Sea back into the Indian Ocean and onto the Red Sea and the Suez Canal.

It took us about four weeks to the Black Sea and Russia. The passage across was beautiful weather all the way. We passed through the Suez Canal and into the Mediterranean Sea, into the Bosphoros

Sea passing Istanbul, past the Dardanelle's and into the Black Sea. We anchored off the port of Kherson for two weeks before we went alongside. We never went to Odessa as the orders changed to go to Kherson. It was a very nice place and we got ashore every night. It was summer time. The country was still communist then and strict with us having to go ashore. We had to be back by 12am but the people were very nice. We arranged football matches with the Russian Navy. We were there for about three weeks and everyone enjoyed themselves. We departed from Russia and sailed to Piraeus, Greece where there was to be a crew changes. We then flew home to Manchester after about five months away.

I was home for a few weeks as I went back to catering college to take a higher grade cookery course at the nautical catering college in Liverpool. Paul Kelly also came up to do his chef/cook's certificate and he stayed at my house. The college was very good and had some of the best teachers, as a lot of them had been chefs and bakers on the old *Cunard* liners: *Queen Elizabeth*, *Queen Mary* and *Caronia*. They certainly knew their stuff and we learnt a lot. There was one teacher there called Billy Byrnes who was always over at the pub during lunch times with us. He was a character. He liked his drink as did we. My course was four weeks and when I finished I went back to sea and joined one of the container ships that ran to the west coast of the states called the *California Star*, sister ship to the *Columbia Star*. I was on there for 12 months. We would be away seven weeks and after a few weeks' leave we either joined or left in Tilbury or Liverpool.

I then went on another container ship, *Blue Star* which was part of the *Act I Associated Container Services*. I joined in Tilbury, London. That was a bit bigger than the *California Star*, built in Germany in about 1969 and it carried a lot of containers. We left Tilbury in June 1977 and went across the East Coat of America, New York, Boston, Philadelphia, Norfolk, Virginia and Charleston through the Panama Canal and to New Zealand where we loaded, then back up to Panama and the USA east coast, back down to New Zealand then across to Australia, Brisbane, Adelaide, Melbourne and Freemantle, across the Indian Ocean through the Suez Canal and to

Piraeus, Greece. The container ship was fast and was in and out of port very quickly. We got four days in Greece when the wine festival was on, so we were up there nearly every night plastered. We finally sailed for Southampton where we went into dry dock and we paid off and went on leave. We had been away about six months, I think.

After a few weeks home I joined another ship, the *Andalucia Star*, one of the 'fruit boats', as we called them. I had to go to Sweden and join it in a place called Halsingborg. I had been there before on the Swedish ship I was on before in 1965 (it was now 1978). I had to fly out to Denmark first, take a train from Copenhagen to Helsingrad and a ferry across to Halsingborg, then a taxi to the ship. I was really hung over from a few days before I had travelled, and when I got on board a party was in full swing. I knew most of the lads so I joined them. The ship had orders for Cape Town to load apples and citrus fruit for Sheerness. As the ship was quite fast it only took over four weeks there and back to Kent. Somehow this ship always had parties at night in the bar and always plenty of women came down in nearly every port. We were in Kent on the River Medway for four days, then got orders to sail to Florida USA where we took general cargo out. We stayed there for a few months between Ecuador, Panama and the States, then we came home with bananas from Ecuador. We docked in Barry Island, South Wales five months later.

That was a good ship – we used to play cards every night for money, and it got too much for some of the lads who had to sign back on again for another voyage as they had lost in cards – but they did not seem to mind. They were a good bunch of lads and we had a good laugh on there. Every Saturday we would have what we called 'pub lunch'. After lunch time we would put out salads and plenty of cold cuts, fish pies and curry and rice and they would just help themselves – officers and crew – and we all got together in the bar or whatever, or went out on deck in the sun for a read. We always got time off, and also in port we would work half days between us. They all carried a chef/steward who was head of the catering department, but in years to come they would be phased out as the crews got smaller and the cook would have to do all the ordering of the stores and the captain gave out the subs and the accounts which were soon to come.

It was coming up to September and after a few weeks home I was to go up to Newcastle to join a new container ship called the *Australia Star*. I forgot to mention but the *Blue Star Line*, owned by the *Vesty Group*, also opened an office in James Street, Liverpool. So we went down there and got our order, or they would ring us up for availability for work. Ken Elliot was our personnel manager and he was very good to us and played a part in getting me home for my mother's funeral, which I never forgot, so I never refused any jobs offered to me. I had no reason to as I liked it in the *Blue Star Line*. Some of my happiest times at sea were when I was there.

It was September 1978 and we had a week getting the ship ready for the maiden voyage. This ship had her own cranes so it could discharge its own containers and load up in small rivers and creeks, off and on to barges. I think that was what it was designed for. Anyway, after everything was ready we got our orders to sail for Auckland, New Zealand via the Panama Canal. We had our last night ashore in Newcastle and sailed the next day. A good passage across the Atlantic Ocean to Cristobal, Panama, took a day to get through. I always like going through the Panama Canal into the many locks there with plenty of scenery. We used to take on an American pilot and once through to the Pacific side he would get off in a launch and we would continue on our way to Auckland. It takes about two weeks or just over. We had a few days in Auckland and we got to see old friends who we'd known over the years of going there. Also we had to prepare special meals for parties for the shippers and we would lay out a big buffet with a hot dish, mostly curry and rice and condiments, with me and the second cook carving all the joints of meat. Lord Vesty himself came down to see the new ship and eat, and other directors and managers of the *Blue Star* fleet. Don't forget they also owned the *Booth Line* which had a service to the Amazon, as well as *Lamport and Holt Line*, South American service, plus a ship they owned in Australia. They also owned a lot of land in Australia and South America, as well as *Lyons* ice cream and *Dewhurst* the butchers – to name a few.

After loading containers we went across to Sydney, Melbourne, Adelaide and Freemantle. We then proceeded across the Indian Ocean to Bombay – this is where the cranes came in handy for discharging the containers and loading them. Afterwards we sailed to Muscat, Oman, Bahrain, Kuwait and Iran, then back to Bombay and we were on our way to Australia and New Zealand as that was the new service it was going on. Another ship called the *New Zealand Star* joined us on that run. We paid off in Kuwait then because we had four months in already and stayed in a hotel overnight and flew home. I was only home for three weeks before flying out to LA to join the *Southland Star*. Paul Kelly's brother John was my second cook and Billy Nolan was mess man. Billy was from Liverpool and John from Nottingham.

That was a really good ship, and a good party ship in port. We were on the crusader run West Coast USA, Canada, Honolulu, Fiji and New Zealand. The *Southland Star* was built about 1960 to carry heavy lifts. It had a stulkan crane of about 250 ton lifting capacity, I think. Anyway, it had been converted to a container ship, and was quite a fast and happy ship. I was on there for six months, joined her in January and came home in June. I have some good memories, particularly of a lot of women who came on board.

One particular incident occurred on there when the ship was in Littleton. We were all having a drink in the British, the pub outside the gate with all the girls, when one of them asked me if I could take her up to Auckland on the ship. Well, after a few beers, I said yes as it was only a short run – two days I think. Anyway, we were all in the crew bar as usual in the ports before we sailed, and I told this one to go down to my cabin, which she duly did. They don't usually search the ship before we sail. Anyway, we left for port and next morning I went up to work in the galley as usual when the chief steward said the captain was doing an inspection. I was surprised because they didn't usually come around when the ship was on the coast. Anyways he did at about 11am the mate came up the galley and said the old man wanted to see me in my room. I went down and there only to find him with the chief steward and Edith, the girl. "You should know better than to take on stowaways," he said, "get up to my room now and bring the young lady with you." He then said, "Chief mate, I know there must be more women on board, search the ship now." Next thing about 15 women appeared from different rooms and lockers. The next one caught with a girl in his cabin was my friend the motorman, Duncan McGillivray from Yorkshire, a real nice bloke. Anyway, the old man was fuming by then. No wonder they found the women, there was underwear hanging on the rails and the ship smelt like a brothel with the perfume! The captain had me and Duncan up on the bridge and said, "I know there are more crew members involved in this matter." Duncan and I said that we were the only ones involved in bringing women on board. He said the police would be in Auckland on arrival, as he had to report the incident. He said to us, "You never involved your shipmate and you took the blame, so for that I admire you both – now go down and look after the girls until we get to port."

When we arrived in Auckland the police came on board and took us all to the police station. Me and Duncan got jailed over night and appeared in court. Aiding and abetting stowaways was the charge. We were in the local papers. Anyway, we came back to the ship the next morning. The lads paid our fine and the captain came to us and shook hands and said, "It's forgotten now so have a drink with me." He was ok and still let girls on board and even brought them drinks. Most captains never brought the girls off the ships then because I think they knew at least the crew were on board the ship and not in trouble ashore. We used to have some good times ashore, especially Honolulu and Fiji Islands, the States and Canada. All the girls in New Zealand and Australia called us the 'poms'. I think it means prisoner of mother England when the Aussies call us that! Really it was the Aussies who were the poms when they where transported out there in the eighteenth century. To this day they still say poms, a bit like the Americans call us limeys, because in the sailing ship days they gave us lime juice for scurvy. Mind you, they gave us lime juice in 1963 when I was on a *Blue Funnel* ship. Once a week we got it. These days on a ship we have bottles of it anytime you want it.

We flew home from LA for crew change. I was home for four weeks then I joined the *Starman Anglia* in Manchester. I was only on it for three weeks, then went up to Middlesbrough and I paid off. That was a small ship but was built for heavy lifts. A few weeks later I flew out to Toronto, Canada to join the *Starman America*, another heavy lift ship. We got orders to go to Algeria. After leaving the lakes and out into the Atlantic a few days later, I was on deck having a cup of tea when I spotted a buoy floating past the ship. I immediately alerted the bridge and the officer of the watch turned the ship around and they retrieved the buoy. When they checked where it had came from I think it was from a German ship that had gone down months before with all hands – no survivors. Anyway, it was sent to Germany when the ship arrived in Liverpool from Algeria. I think the ship that went down was called the *Munchen*, if I am not mistaken.

I was to join one of the *Lamport and Holt* ships, the *Boswell*, all named after painters, and it was an SD14 make and built in 1979 in Newcastle, I think. Anyway, the design went back to the 1950s and *Lamport and Holt* got four of them, including *Browning, Belloc* and *Bronte*. The run was to Brazil and Argentina. I did two trips in her from November to March 1980.

Chapter 5
Off to the Falkland Islands

They were nice ships and the crew were all good lads: Jimmy McKeon, second steward, Chris Harrison the second cook from York, Peter Jones on deck, Davey Jones a steward from North Wales, Jimmy Boffey, an ordinary seaman. The Chief Steward, Jimmy Spears, was a really nice man. He got a football team organised on board. He was our manager so on the way down to Brazil we all used to go down the hatch and practice. We had a few games in Brazil and Argentina – it was a good laugh too.

Jimmy Spears died a few years ago in 2006. I think I was away and missed the funeral. I sailed with Jimmy on numerous voyages, he was a gentleman. The captain was Hughes who had his wife on board. A nice man, and fair. When we would be coming back at 5am for work he used to say to us, "Here's the dawn patrol back." The Brazilian coast was great, with plenty of bars and women.

On the way down to Brazil I got an infection in my ears – the mastoids. It was really bad. I was in the ship's hospital for a week and the captain had to get instructions on how to treat me as we were still at sea, seven days from the Brazilian coast. I was getting injections every day from the old man and I was off work for ten days in the ship's hospital. I was soon on my feet again when we arrived at Rio de Janeiro and saw the doctor who checked me out. After that ship I went down to Cape Town and back on the *Andalusian Star* to load apples for the UK, only away five weeks, then I went back to the *Californian Star* for three trips to the west coast of the USA from July 1980 to January 1981. Then in February I went back in the ACT I – we were away for seven months, running between the east coast of America to New Zealand to Australia. We came home via Suez after going out via Panama. It was August 1981 and we had just missed the riots around the country and Liverpool.

I came home with one of the firemen off the ship, a black man from the south end of Liverpool. He was well into his sixties and a character. Born and bread in Liverpool, he had been at sea all his life and he could tell some stories. He went through the Second World War in the convoys, got torpedoed three times and still went back out to sea. We tend to forget the contribution these brave merchant seamen of all race and colour went through. Only for them, as well as other armed forces, we would not be here today enjoying the life that we have. Thank you, Dick and your comrades.

We got a lift home off a lorry driver going up to Liverpool from Southampton – Dick knew his family, and we gave him a few bob for the lift. I was home for a few months. After that I must have been working by the ships in Liverpool or around the country – you never got a stamp in your discharge book unless you signed on and sailed. Your seaman book is basically all your life, so you can relate to where you were on certain dates. All you had to do was just look in your discharge books – I can go back years, and it has also helped me to write my story.

On December 1981 I joined the *Starman America* up in Granton Firth of Forth. We were there over Christmas and had a good time with the locals ashore who invited us all up to their house on Boxing Day. Billy Anderson was on there, and John Moran. It only carried one cook, same as *Starman Anglia*, as it only had a crew of twelve. I met a girl called Isobel while the ship was there and kept in touch – I went up to see her a year later. We went up to Peterhead, north east Scotland, with a big articulated lorry that had a big transformer on it. It had to have a police escort all the way from Yorkshire. It took a few days for it to get up to Granton. After that we sailed to Dunkirk. I got relived by Jimmy Jordan, an old cook and friend, as I was going back to the *Starman Anglia* in Liverpool. January 1982 we were going out to a place in Mexico, Lorenzo Gardinas, on the west coast of the Pacific Ocean.

We took on stores and were due to sail in a few days. The catering superintendent came on board to make sure I had everything, I asked him for a half day and could Eddie Owen, the shore side chef, come down and stand in for me before the voyage. He said sure, go ahead. Eddie Owen was a bit of a character – he never had a cigarette out of his mouth, he went away for years and had about six daughters, so he decided to come ashore and get the job as work-by cook. He did all the parties for the shippers and Lord Vesty, and relieved us cooks when we came back from deep sea. It could be any port in the UK or continent – Eddie would be there. Everyone knew him and he trained a lot of the young lads up who are cooks today.

Anyway, Eddie came down and I went off to my usual haunt for a drink, the *Yankee Clipper*. All the seamen went there between 3 and 6 o'clock after the pubs closed. It was run by Sonny Phillips – he was ok with all the lads, and you could always get a drink off him. The next morning I turned to the galley and made breakfast. John Moran joined that day as AB. The old man got a bit annoyed because I never told him I was off on half-day.

We left Liverpool and proceeded to Panama Canal and then up to Mexico by Baja, California, discharged, then went down to Sydney, Australia, were there a few days and then got orders for Kobe, Japan. Loaded there, then back down to a place in Java called Cilicap, then back up to Singapore. We were there about a week. Singapore is a really beautiful place, very clean and the airport is one of the best I've seen. At the time it was very modern. I flew home from Singapore with a few of the lads I knew. We were away for five months.

While we were away the Falklands War had started. While we were away the *Blue Star Line* had got the ex New Zealand ferry *Rangatira* which used to run between Littleton and Wellington before it came to England. Anyway, *Blue Star* had it turned into a troopship – it was to carry various regiments to Port Stanley. She was fitted out in Devonport Docks in Plymouth and I was to join it there as head chef. So, after a brief spell home, I was off to Devonport along with a lot of lads from Liverpool to get it ready for sea. We were billeted in the royal navy barracks for about ten days then we went around to Southampton to take on troops – over a 1,000 I think – mostly royal engineers, RAF personnel and also a naval party on board along with a commander – so there were a lot of people to feed! We had chief petty officer, chef royal navy and I, cook and two other naval cooks. The Royal Navy was there to help us with the numbers and to guide us as they had served on aircraft carriers. I had two second cooks, about eight assistant cooks, two lads who just peeled potatoes all day and two bakers. Later on in that trip, just before I was to go home, Terry Flaherty and Davey Griffiths arrived down in Port Stanley with Tony Caddock, who was an excellent baker, along with Bob Reid, who had been baker on the two queens *Cunard* passenger ships. Davey and Terry were second cooks.

When we left Southampton the Argentinians had surrendered, so it was all over by then and the troops we had were to help rebuild Stanley, so the *Rangatira* was used as a hotel ship for them until suitable accommodation was ready. They went ashore in the morning and came back for dinner, so we still had to cater for large numbers. We used to go ashore now and again, but there was nothing there, very desolate. One afternoon we walked up to Tumble Down Mountain where the Scots guards fought against the Argentinians. There was a cross dedicated to the dead. It took us a few hours there and back – how those soldiers did it with all their packs I don't know. Time seemed to drag down there where there were lots of British ships. The Royal Navy were waiting on the phantom jets to arrive from the UK for Port Stanley Airfield, just in case of another attack by Argentina, which was highly unlikely by now as they were completely demoralised.

Five months later I came home on the *Norland*, another North Sea Ferry requisitioned for the war. Her job now, after bringing the Paratroop Regiment down to Port Stanley to fight, was to bring personnel from Ascension Island to the Falklands and back along with another ship, the ex-hospital ship *Uganda*. I think it took us two weeks from Stanley to Ascension Island then on to an air force plane VC 10, home to Brize Norton, England. I was glad to get home – a bit exhausted – and my dad and family were glad to see me.

I had a month home. I was in the *Yankee Clipper* most afternoons, like all the seamen. I got a call to join another ship, the *Starman Anglia*, and I was to join her in a place called Oskarshamn, Sweden. It was 11th November and we went to Finland to load cargo for Beaumont, Texas. I came home the end of January from Texas. I was home for four weeks and found myself going back to the *Rangatira* in Port Stanley. We flew from Brize Norton to Ascension Island and sailed down on British India's *Uganda*. One of my second cooks was a Somali man named Mohammed, a good cook – they all loved his curry and rice. I still see him sometimes – last time I went up to visit him in the Somali club off Princes Park, where he still cooks the curry for the Somali people.

I spent four months there and came back on the *Uganda* to Ascension Island and a VC 10 to Brize Norton. I must have stayed home a bit longer than I usually did. I must have been working by the ships in the UK because my next voyage was not until October, and that was back down to the Falkland Islands on the *Avelona Star*. As I said earlier in my book, I took her on the maiden voyage years before. I joined that in Portsmouth and sailed down to Port Stanley. Terry Flaherty and Dave Griffiths were my second cooks, and we were in Port Stanley for Christmas and had a good time. Christmas Day is always a lot to do on a ship, but we soon got everything ready and we were in port not at sea. December in the Falklands is summer time and it was really nice. Coming back to Ascension Island the weather was really bad – it was hard to cook and the ship rolled and tossed for days, a force 10 I remember, but once in Ascension Islands we had nice weather. We arrived back in Portsmouth at the end of January and I was home for about two months – unusual for me. I joined the *ACT I* container ship in April and went out to Australia and New Zealand via the Panama Canal and back via the Suez Canal in July – we arrived back in Tilbury.

The next ship I joined was the *ACT 7* which was one of the newer container ships, a lot bigger than the other ACT ships and faster. I went down to Tilbury to join her – Dave Griff was second cook. We sailed over to Bremen for four weeks in a dry dock. It was ok over there – we were ashore every night, then we came back to

Tilbury to load containers for Australia and New Zealand. When we arrived in Tilbury I found out a captain was coming who I had not got on with years before on a previous ship, so I told the mate and chief steward I did not want to sail with the ship. The mate said he would not remember me from way back, as he liked his drink. The superintendent came on and said to me that I was to sail and he would go up and see the captain. Later on he came down and said to me, "I've had a word with the captain and you will be sailing, and no problems from either of you." So that was settled, we sailed the next day via Cape Town.

I think we had Christmas at sea somewhere in Australia or New Zealand – anyway, Christmas morning just before 12 o'clock the old man invited the catering crew to his cabin for a drink. I was not really up for going but along we went with the chief steward. Come in, the old man shouted, well on the way! Anyway, he gave us a drink then he kept asking if he had sailed with me before. I said, "Maybe, I can't remember." I did because it was a big row about six years before on a ship in the Persian Gulf. Anyway, he started on the second cook, Dave Griff, and asked, "When am I going to get a chocolate pudding off you second cook?" I could see what was coming and Davey was a good cook and baker – very good on Chinese food, having learnt off the old Chinese cooks in *Lamport and Holt's* ship. So I said, "Come on, let's go," so we left the cabin and he shouted, "Chocolate sauce." Dave looked at me laughing saying, "I will give him chocolate sauce and pudding" – I won't say no more, he never asked again. Dave had to go home from New Zealand, domestic problems and Trevor Jones came out to replace him. Another good cook who served his time in *Blue Funnel Line*, he was married to Teresa and had three lads – a nice family. It was a good trip and we got no more out of the old man. I had a steward, Andy May as my second cook for a few days until Trevor came out to New Zealand to join the ship. John Moran was on there, Jimmy Murtah second steward from Bradford; (funny he was), Brian Mather, AB Will Gilkes (a West Indian AB). One of my friends, Benny Byrnes, who was an ex-seaman, went ashore and started sea tax years ago – well, his brother Jimmy came down with his wife and kids, and we had some good parties at night in New Zealand. Sadly Jimmy died a few years ago. Pat Higgins, a motorman, was on there, Billy McGill the motorman and Brian French AB from Portsmouth. We came back via the Panama Canal in February. When I see Dave Griff and Pat Higgins we always bring up, "Remember the voyage on the *ACT 7*."

As I said before, being at sea is a lot different to shore side, and of course you get bad times but the good times outweigh the bad. You meet a lot of friends through the years at sea. Some you keep in touch with and some you don't. I can remember names from my first trip to sea in 1962 but in 2008 I find it hard to remember names from the last trip. When anyone asks me where I was ten years ago, I just look back in my seaman's discharge book and it is all recorded, with the time and place I joined the ship and the time and place I left. Really, all of your life's work is in the book – I am on my third seaman's book now.

I was home a few months before I joined the *Scottish Star*, a reefer ship on her second voyage. I joined her in New Haven, May 1985, and sailed down to Gisbon, New Zealand to load a cargo of kiwi fruits for Zeebrugge, Belgium. After we discharged cargo we sailed to Cape Town to load oranges and apples. Gisbon in New Zealand is a nice little place. There is a statue of Captain James Cook on the mountain overlooking the bay where he landed on his ship over 200 years ago. We were there for a few days. On the way back from New Zealand we hit bad weather in the Caribbean. Just after leaving the Panama Canal, and the cargo of kiwi fruit smashed in the side hold. These things happen and reefer ships like this roll a lot anyway. I was home two months and I went over to Belfast to join another newly built reefer ship called the *English Star*. We were over in Belfast for about five days, then sailed on sea trials before sailing off to New Zealand in January 1986. We went to Tauranga and loaded mutton for Odessa, Russia. We got to Odessa about the end of February/beginning of March. I remember it was bitterly cold. We came around Australia by Hobart, Tasmania into the Indian Ocean and through the Suez Canal, then into the Bosporus Sea, past Istanbul and into the Black Sea. Ten years before I was in a port just up from Odessa and it was summer time, really hot. We were there for two weeks and went ashore to the seamen's club for a few beers or Champagne, as it was so cheap there. The man in charge was very friendly and very proud of his country, Russia which was still a communist state. I met an old Italian man who was living in Odessa – he spoke good English and I asked him how he came to be in Russia. He told me he had fought for the Russians in the Second World War against the Germans, and he decided to stay. He told me he received a pension and was quite happy there where he had married a Russian girl and had grown up children. I got to see a lot of Odessa.

One day the captain came down to the galley to see me. Captain McKillop was a gentleman. He had invited some people from the seamen's club for dinner one night and asked me to cook a meal, which I did, and they enjoyed it. Anyway, they asked the captain would he come up to the club the next day and talk to teachers and students from the Odessa State University about the UK. Captain McKillop was not one for talking so he asked me, "Eddie, would you mind going to the seaman's club to speak to the people from the university?" I was a bit hesitant at first but I gave in as the captain was a nice man. So the next night I went up to the club. Some of the lads off our ship came up to hear what I was going to talk about.

When I arrived there that evening the place was packed out with young and old alike. There were rows of people sitting down. I had told the staff at the club that the captain could not make it as he had to stay on the ship and was sorry he could not come, so I would do it – they were delighted. The man told me that the teachers and students wanted to know all about me, as well as the UK. There were also a few professors in the audience, as I was to find out after my speech. I got onto the stage a little nervous but was ok after a few questions, which included questions on Liverpool getting bombed during the war. I replied back speaking slowly – I had told the audience before I started that I hoped they understood me as my accent was not like the English they learnt. I told the audience the stories my mother told me – going into the air raid shelter, a lot of people getting killed, the city and the docks reduced to rubble, along with other cities in the UK, and I told them that Russia took the brunt of the German invasion and came through losing many people in their struggle. That seemed to strike a chord with them and they started to applaud.

Before I knew it I had been up on the podium speaking for nearly an hour and started to enjoy myself. "Had I met the Beatles?" they asked me. They were wonderful people. After I finished speaking, I mingled with them all, talking and having a snack and drinks, when one man came onto the podium and spoke out over the microphone to us all. "Citizens of USSR, I would like your attention for a moment." He then called me up and said, "We would like to thank you for your fine speech in front of students and teachers from the Odessa State University tonight, and would like to present you with this book on Odessa." I got a fantastic reception and applause and I thanked them all for listening, and hoped that one day we might meet again in a more peaceful world. I don't think Richard Burton could have done better! Then one of the students got up and finished the night off by playing John Lennon's 'Imagine'. Inside the book is written: 'This book was presented to Edward Bolton in memory of his speech to the students and teachers of Odessa University 1985.' My old friend Joe Lewin, a cook who passed away in 2006, used to say I was the first person to help bring *glasnost*.

The next day the captain came down and said, "Well done Eddie, I heard all about your speech." I enjoyed my time there. After we discharged the cargo, we got orders to sail for South Africa to load citrus fruit and it was to be my last trip in the *Blue Star Line*. After 14 years there, I needed a change. We arrived back in Sheerness, Kent from Cape Town at the end of October 1985. Times where changing in 1985. Within shipping there were not so many companies left and those that were employed cheaper foreign crew and in the next year the shipping federation would be closing for good. This meant we had to find our own jobs through agencies when previously the shipping federation found us jobs. On top of which container ships were getting bigger and needed less crew – a big change was on the way.

I was home for eight months, the longest I have ever been home. It was not easy finding a ship again. I started to drink a lot more than I had done before. I drank when I came home but was away in a few weeks. I never drank at sea, only in port. My father was getting a bit worried about my drinking – he was not used to seeing me drink so much and spend all my money on drink, plus the fact that I was getting over a relationship with a girl I was very fond of, so that never helped me. It went on for a while and I managed to get myself on course. I told my dad I had a job – he was relieved I think that I was back at work. Anyway, I was to join a *BP* tanker and was flying out to Borneo in December 1986. There were six tankers all at anchor. They had been there fully loaded with crude oil since the Iraq and Iran war. Each ship was nearly 300,000 ton – very big. I was to be out in Borneo, not once getting ashore, as we were miles from the coast. However we had everything we needed – a gym, cinema and plenty of fishing. Hugh Carragher, AB from Bootle was on there, as well as John Duffy. We flew out via Hong Kong to Brunei from Gatwick. Mark Quillam was the steward who came out with me. Hughie was already on board and John Duffy was to follow a month later. We had a good crew on there. I was in the gym at night when I finished work and either went fishing or watched a movie. The weather was beautiful. We caught tuna and king clip, which we cooked. We had stores come out from Singapore every month. A lot of sharks were caught – most times they would break the line. I don't believe in killing just for the sake of it. A lot of the lads felt the same way, so we let a lot of fish go and ate what we caught.

Christmas was very good on there. We cooked dinner about 1 o'clock and put out a buffet in the afternoon so we were able to celebrate. I never drank a beer the whole time I was on there. I was feeling fit and had a good suntan on me. We used to play cricket on the deck every Saturday afternoon as we were on half-day, and visit the other ships to play, put down the lifeboat to go across to the other ships. Everybody used to enjoy that. We had a lot of balls, as a lot used to go over the side! My seven months on there was coming to an end and I paid off and went off the ship in a launch to Brunei. It was June 1987.

We flew to Singapore on *Royal Brunei Airlines* top class. Instead of going straight home I stayed in Singapore for a week. I forgot to mention I had moved out of my dad's house and bought a house in Runcorn. That was in 1986. I don't know why I moved there, I never liked it. I was in Liverpool more, it was just an investment. I was to stay there until 1992 when I moved back to Liverpool.

After I came off the *BP* tanker I went on a diving support ship in Peterhead. I was only on it for two weeks. That year my father died in hospital in Runcorn. I buried him from my house there. That was 1987. He had been ill for some time since my mother died. He had retired but was never the same. He had emphysema, and although he smoked he always said he got a bad chest when he was in Burma in the Second World War. He was always fixing cars, lying on the wet road in all kinds of weather without warm clothes on. That's the way they were, people his age. He was 66 when he died. We were all at the hospital before he died – he was slipping into a coma and that night my sister rang me to say that he had passed away. It was a very sad time. He is buried with my mother in Allerton Cemetery. I go up and take flowers to the grave which is kept really nice. The loss of my dad affected us all, but like he used to say, do all you can in life and make the best of it, you are a long time dead. He used to come out with some sayings – I would be driving past the cemetery with him and he would say to me, "That's one appointment we can't get out of." "What's that?" I would say, and he would just nod over there to the cemetery. He was well liked by everyone.

Before he died his mother passed away. She lived in North Wales and we used to visit her a lot. She was 83 when she died. That hit him as well, he loved her very much. His sister Doreen was at the funeral. Margaret, the youngest of his sisters, lived in the states – she was not there and Annie and Kathleen were not there but sent their condolences. Annie was ill herself. Having lost two husbands she was very upset over my dad as they were very close as kids growing up in London. Kathleen was away on holiday when he died.

In January 1988 I got a job with a Danish company, *Maersk Tankers*. They were British flagged ships in the Isle of Man. I went over there for an interview for a chief cook's job and, to my surprise, I had to fly out the next day to a place in Sicily called Malazzo where I joined the product tanker *Maersk Neptune*. I joined it with a steward as there was only 18 crew and two of us catering. We sailed to the Black Sea Port of Romania Constanza loading black oil for New Jersey, USA, back to the Mediterranean, Marseille, south of France, Algeria and back to Long Island, USA. We had a bit of a collision in New Jersey with another ship – not serious but we had a few days in port which gave us a chance to visit New York. We went to a place in Saudi Arabia called Yanbu in the Red Sea where we loaded oil for Japan. After that we came down to Singapore where I signed off the ship. I had an open ticket so I spent a few days in Singapore before going home. Singapore is a lovely place and every time I go back there they are reclaiming land and building more apartments – it really is a lovely place. I still go there now. I love the place, it's somewhere where people are brought up with respect from when they are young. Some people say that Singapore laws are too militaristic. I disagree. As long as you abide by the law and respect them, you will not get in any trouble. The people there are a mixture of all races and religions and they get on well. It's a country that others could learn a lot from.

I had been away six months when I received a call to join a ship out in Koper, Yugoslavia. I got my flight details and flew out to Trieste in northern Italy. Then the agent picked me up and we drove to Kopea to join the ship. The journey took four hours and the scenery was lovely, passing through villages and mountains, stopping for refreshments. I eventually arrived on board the ship in the afternoon. The ship was the same as the last one. It was called the *Maersk Nimrod*, so we were going to the same ports as before – the Mediterranean, Black Sea and across to the States. We went to some lovely places on the USA east coast – Providence, Rhode Island and Northville. We then went over to Milford Haven, South Wales and loaded a cargo of aviation fuel for Chiba, Japan. That took us five weeks to get there. I had been on that ship for seven months. I liked it on these ships – not a lot of crew, only 18 as I said, with plenty of food stores. I was responsible for ordering these, which kept everyone happy.

I paid off the ship on my birthday 25th January 1989 in Japan. Before I came off, I asked the captain to fax the company to see if they would give me an open ticket as I planned to travel around Asia for a few weeks. To my surprise, they said yes. So I got a flight down to Singapore from Tokyo and had a few days there. The company gave me a list of hotels where I could get a discount. I then went down to Bali in Indonesia for a week. I fell asleep on the beach. It was not very sunny, but I got a little bit burnt and I was red raw so had to take it easy. I don't usually lie down in the sun, preferring to walk around. Anyway, I came back up to Singapore, had a week there then flew home. The only air fare I paid for was from Singapore to Bali and back.

It was getting to the end of February and very cold. I was living in Runcorn until March before getting a call to join another oil tanker called the *Maersk Navarine*. I was to fly out to New York to join it in New Jersey. By then I had got to see the crews again I had sailed with previously. Alan Banks, the bosun, was there but only for a short spell. He was paying off. I knew his brother Bobby, a cook from the *Blue Star*. On that ship we stayed out running between the east coast of America to the Caribbean – some lovely places such as St Eustacious, small islands, Curacao, Barbados, Dutch Antilles – we even went through the Panama Canal to Los Angeles, but our boson was killed in a tragic accident whilst tying the ship up on the buoys offshore. All I remember was Mick Kadilac, the bosun, came in the galley just before tea and asked me to put his dinner off on the side because he was going to help the lads tie up on the buoys. Anyway the rope on the manifold centre of the tanker came up and hit Mick across the chest causing massive bleeding. He died on his way to the hospital in the helicopter. Mick was a nice man and was missed by all.

We were there a few days and a new bosun came out. Tommy Yates from Liverpool, another nice man – you got a good laugh from Tommy. I was seeing this girl at home and Tommy had been out with her. We were also talking about this club and the girl who worked there. I said I knew her and Tommy said he went out with her but she had left him for some cook. I asked Tommy who it was and he said he didn't know but that he went away on long trips. I said, "Oh you can't trust these women Tom." "You are right," he said. We had a good trip on there and came home from New York in August. I was home for about six weeks as I went on a bakers and confectioners course and to my city and guilds in catering.

After that I went out to Houston, Texas to join the *Maersk Javelin*, another tanker. We sailed from there in November 1989 to Chiba Japan where I paid off in January 1990.It was not a long trip as they wanted me to join another ship, a gas carrier in the UK. I did not mind though, we were still on pay, so in March I joined the ship *Maersk Capitan* in Teesport and we sailed across the Atlantic to Houston Texas to load gas for Belgium and the UK. I paid off in Houston the end of May and flew home for a few weeks. Then I flew out to Cagliari to join another tanker, the *Maersk Gannet*. We were on charter to the MOD taking oil down to the Falkland Islands from Italy and Sicily. I was on there four months and paid off in Sicily and flew home. I had a bit of a disagreement with the old man over store. Normally they never bothered you, but this one was cutting back. I ended up resigning, but the company kept the back door open for me as these things happen. I left and went and got a job on one of the nuclear boats, *James Fishers Ltd*. I was on there over a week and left, then went back to *Maersk* – it was a good company and treated me well. I was sorry I left them. I realised then but we all make mistakes and must move on. I forgot to mention that I worked on a couple of oil rigs in the North Sea and years later in West Africa as a night cook/baker but it never appealed to me at all.

The next job I got was on the *Pacific Swan*, one of the nuclear ships out of Barrow belonging to British nuclear fuels but managed by *James Fishers & Son*. I only worked by a couple of weeks in December 1990, I then went on the sludge boat *Consortium* for just three weeks relief work out of Liverpool to the coast of North Wales. I got a job on a ship called the *Norse Lagan*, a passenger and RO ship – it was a Dutch registered ship with Dutch officers and

Philippine crew and British lads. I was chief cook and we sailed between Liverpool and Belfast. We carried a lot of lorries travelling over from Ireland to Europe. Then after a while we started to get a lot of foot passengers. I was on there six months and we worked a two week on two week off.

After I left there I went down to Southampton to join the Norse Mersey, which was quite an old ferry, and after coming out of dry dock we sailed up to Liverpool to go on the Belfast to Liverpool run. I was on there for a short stay.

I wanted to go back to deep sea and got a phone call saying I had a job with *P&O* container ships as a chief cook. I was happy and in 1992 I flew out to Piraeus to join the *Nedlloyd Tasman*, a container ship in which we sailed to Australia and New Zealand. The job was ok, I had a second cook and two stewards, I think. We came back to La Spezia in Italy where I came off in January. I found that the ships were getting less time in port, not like years before when you had plenty of time. Containerisation changed all that and as the years progressed it was getting to a matter of hours on port.

It was the first time I came across Ernie Rankin in *P&O* containers since 1963 when I sailed with him on the *Blue Funnel* ship the *Menestheus*. He was now in the crewing department of *P&O* containers. I think Ernie was with the *Blue Funnel* up until they went to ocean fleets. The first container ships where beautiful and big at that time in the early 1970s, the Tokyo Bay class, which I will come to later.

I was home a few days and I went to join the *Resolution Bay*, a bigger container ship than the *Nedlloyd Tasman*. I got on the train down to Tilbury to join it in February 1993. It was a three month round trip to Australia and New Zealand via the Cape Of Good Hope stopping at Cape Town. I had not been in Cape Town since 1986 so there had been big changes – a beautiful place with a fantastic view when you are out at sea passing it. We had about 12 hours there then proceeded to Freemantle, Western Australia. We had a good crew on there. My second cook was Russ Kujack from Widnes, a young lad. Tommy Irvine was one of the stewards from Greenock, another nice man and funny with his quick Clydeside wit. The passage was good across the Indian Ocean and afternoons were spent out on deck reading as the catering was from 1 o'clock until 3. That lovely blue sea and sky, you cannot beat it.

A funny thing I forgot to mention – after we left Tilbury and once in the Bay of Biscay, the weather was a bit rough. Anyway, a pigeon flew on board. It must have got lost, as it had a ring on its leg, I think a racing pigeon from Spain. It stayed with us for four weeks just sitting outside by the engine room fan which was warm, especially after leaving Cape Town as you go south about to Australia and really cold weather and strong winds. It was well fed and put on a lot of weight – it looked like a large chicken. On arrival in Freemantle it just flew off that morning. So I thought no more of it as we took on our stores – fresh veg and engine and deck stores. After lunch I decided to go ashore for a half-day as we worked it between us in different ports. Anyway, I was walking past the park in Freemantle just by Cliff Street, I think, and there on the grass was the pigeon along with other pigeons. I bet the owner would have been surprised, the pigeon making its way to Western Australia. It would have been a good story for all those pigeon fans. You could not mistake it for its size, it's a wonder it got off the ground to fly!

After Freemantle we went around to Adelaide. We arrived there in the evening and an old friend of mine, John Lamb, came down to see me with his son. John had just retired from sea; his last job was motorman on the tugs in Adelaide. John was from a big family from the south end of Liverpool – Sussex Gardens, I think – a lot of seamen are from that area and it is a really close knit community. John told me a bit of his life story, which I found really interesting. He went to sea during the war as a young boy, as a lot did at the outbreak of World War Two. The ship John was on got torpedoed by a German submarine off Crete and sank and John, along with other survivors, were in the lifeboat when they were picked up by the Germans and taken to hospital. In the next bed to John was the German boxer Max Schelling who was a wounded German soldier. John said he was a great man to talk to and John, being a great boxing fan, was enthralled by him. The next stop for John was

Germany where he spent the rest of the war in a German prisoner of war camp. On being released after hostilities ceased, John went back to sea. I asked him how he came to live in Australia, which was another sad episode, as I will continue.

John met a young woman in Liverpool and they fell deeply in love with each other, but there was just one barrier – religion. John was from a predominately Catholic part of the south end and the girl was from the Protestant area, which was the top end of Park Road – the family were staunch Orange Lodge. In those days it was very bitter. Her family did not want her to marry John and John's family were the same. When John was at sea he would write to her and her him, but she never received most of John's letters as her parents destroyed them to break them up. John then was on a ship out in Australia. He eventually jumped ship, as we called it, and decided to settle in Australia and wrote time and again to the girl in Liverpool to come out and join him. She never got the letters. It was very sad but that was the way it was in those days – not so much now, but it still goes on. I believe John was always a ladies man in his younger days and had all the women after him. He had that certain charm about him still. He can play the piano, accordion and sing like Satchmo Louis Armstrong. If you are out with John he always gets up and sings. He is in his late eighties now.

We had two nights in Adelaide, which was unusual for us, and John took me and Tommy Irvine out in different pubs. We met all his friends and then we invited them down to the ship and gave them something to eat. Tommy really enjoyed himself and thought a lot of John Lamb. John was to later to come over to the UK and I took him up to the retired seamen's club off Vauxhall Road, the Eldonian Centre, where John got up and sang. He was given a standing ovation. A lot of people came up to him asking whether he knew their dad or uncle in Australia – John knew everyone. He loved being amongst all the old seafarers. He was in his seventies and was still chatting up the ladies. We could not get John to leave.

After we left Adelaide we went to Melbourne, another nice city, then around to Sydney. We docked in what was previously called Port Botany. It is not so far from the city itself, about half-an-hour by tax. It is a big container base there now. Before we tied up just after Sydney Bridge at a place called Ballmayne, and we could walk into the town and a lot of old friends I knew from the past came on board. Rose, an Aboriginal girl who I knew from the 1970s, was married to Alastair, an English lad who jumped ship years before. They got married and had three children, all girls. She told me she was divorced from Alastair and she was having problems with one of her daughters who was addicted to drugs – they were lovely children and they sent me pictures of them at school, so I was their 'Uncle Eddie'. I was sorry to hear that, but Rose was a strong girl. She would say to me, "Eddie, she chose that path; we have tried to help her but no avail." It's a scourge worldwide, so many young people now on drugs. Until they start to bring in Draconian measures and give longer sentences to drug baron's and dealers, this misery to family's will continue. I have not seen Rose since, or Alastair, but when I retire I hope to make a journey to catch up with friends out in Australia and New Zealand.

After we left Sydney we went across to Auckland, New Zealand for one night in, then down to Wellington to spend one night there. I also had friends down in both ports, it was always nice to see them. Then we went down to the south island to Lyttleton, another place I like, and an old friend of mine I met there, Donald McIntyre from Barra, one of the islands of Scotland. I sailed with him in the *New Zealand Star* and *Act 1*, but I had not seen him in 15 years. He had packed in and went out there to live and work, but he came on board. Dave Holbrook was an AB on our ship – a bit of a character Dave, he has a twin brother, a cook, and you cannot tell the difference between the two. He and Donald went on the ale in the British. I went on and met them that evening in the British, a pub well known in New Zealand. I had many a good night there – a lot of seamen retired now will remember the British pub in Lytton. Our last port of call was Port Chalmers in the Southern Hemisphere, a nice little town with a few pubs outside the gate.

A night in there and we sailed for the UK via Cape Horn around South America, and the route we took was very cold, with winds and big waves with the ship rolling around. After about two weeks we came around Cape Horn still blowing a gale and altered course for north. As we progressed along the weather started to get better with blue sky and blue seas. After a week we were in the tropics, not far off the Brazilian coast. We went ahead until we came to the Canary Islands, truly a lovely sight with the islands sticking out of the sea. We never stopped and a few days later we entered the Bay of Biscay – sometimes the weather is bad and sometimes it is like a millpond, it all depends. It was not so bad and we finally arrived in Tilbury, London docks 12 weeks after we left there. In the 1950s, '60s and '70s on the old ships that trip would have been five months, maybe more, as the ships were not containerised then as they are today. So therefore it took longer to load and discharge the cargo and also they were a lot slower speed – but you liked it better then as you got longer in port. The Merchant Navy was changing drastically, fewer ships with British crews, faster and far less time in port. This was the 1990s.

The next ship I was to join in the summer of 1993 was one of the new *P&O* container ships getting built at the time, the *Jervis Bay*. There was only a crew of 18, I think. I joined that one in Southampton as that was where all the ships going to the Far East sailed from, and docked on the way home. This class of ship was big – 50,000 tonne gross and over 20 knot speed. We sailed from the UK via the Suez Canal calling at Jeddah, Saudi Arabia in the Red Sea then on to Port Klang, Malaysia for a few hours in then on to Singapore, Hong Kong, Taiwan, Pusan, Korea, then a few ports in Japan calling back at the same ports on the way back – including Colombo, Sri Lanka, through the Suez Canal, Rotterdam then Southampton. A seven or eight week round trip. Four weeks later I joined the *Singapore Bay*, another new ship, and sailed to the same places coming home on 11th November 1993.

After a brief spell at home I joined another container ship, the *Peninsula Bay*. It was not as new as the last two but modern and fast. I joined in Southampton as we were going out to the Far East. We were in Southampton for a few days and George Mooney was the boson – a nice man, he used to be on the *Elder Dempster Line* ships, the *Aureole* and *Accra* out of Liverpool to West Africa and back. He was from Liverpool and he lived on the south coast somewhere with his wife and family. His wife Sylvia had been a hairdresser on the *Aureole*.

The cable ship *Nexus* was tied up nearby and I met a few of the lads I had sailed with on the *Blue Star Line* in the seamen's mission in Southampton, which was where the seamen went for a drink of an evening and a chat – you always met someone from the past there. Bobby Banks was chief cook on the Nexus and again his brother was bosun. I sailed with Alan in *Maersk Line* tankers. Phil Waddell, his cousin, was their motorman and Charlie Savage from Belfast was the other cook. We had a few drinks in the mission and I invited them over to our ship as we had a bar on board. I think their ship was dry – no beer on board at all, so they enjoyed themselves.

We sailed the next day to the same ports as before. When we got to Kobe, Japan after discharging the containers, the ship got orders to sail down to a place in the Inland Sea of Japan called Aioi, where in the shipyard they were to take off the bridge to put in more accommodation under it so it could carry more cargo. No sooner had the ship tied up alongside the shipyard than workers swarmed aboard and started to take off the bridge. Within hours the company had decided to fly us home and keep just a few officers on board for the few weeks the ship was in dry dock. It was in the evening we left the ship and got on a bullet train to Kobe, stayed in a hotel overnight and going up to Osaka for our flight home for a few weeks. Then we flew back out to Aioi to pick up the ship and bring the ship home after completion of the bridge deck. The *Peninsula Bay* was a nice ship and I enjoyed my time on there.

I had just filled in my second discharge seaman's book and needed to get a new one. It is your record of sea service, the ships you have served on and dates you left and joined ships – a kind of record of your life. I can always tell where I was on a certain date. You give it to the captain on joining and he stamps it and gives you it back on completion of the voyage.

I was always in the seamen's union from when I first joined in 1962 – even when I sailed on Swedish ships I joined the Swedish seamen's union and on returning to British ships joined the National Seamen's Union again. It is now called RMT Rail Maritime and Transport Union. You do really need a union, as without them we would not have the pay and conditions we have today. I've had my views on some things they do and disagree, but that's what it is all about. The only way to sort out things you are not happy with is to go to your branch meetings and have your say. I go to the BGM's when I am home and it is held every two years. Our next one will be in Belfast. Branch Secretary Micky McQuaid will arrange it all, and he is a cook on the Larne to Cairn Ryan Ferry Service and has been at sea a long time. He comes from a big seafaring family, along with many other families with deep traditions of the sea, and his son Danny is a chief officer.

Sadly the membership is dwindling at sea now, coinciding with the sharp decline in the Merchant Navy, and a lot of the seamen today are not in the union and won't join — yet they are willing to take the same pay rise and conditions as us without paying union dues. When I first went out to sea, first thing was to join the union. If you were not up to date you had to pay or no job. Now the laws have changed, and now you don't have to be in a union, but that's the way it is. These things we have today were not given to us, they were fought for by seamen before us. The second thing you did when signing articles was leave your mother an allotment every week. They were the good values drilled into you, and even when I came home off a voyage, especially a long one, I would give my mother money. I used to always say to my mother, "Here you are Mum go and rig yourself out," meaning buy some clothes for yourself. She was always there for me — she brought me up along with my sisters and brother. I got great pleasure in giving the money to her, and it was always there if you were home a long time, as it was not the case with me a lot obviously. The married lads could not do that, but I'm sure they occasionally did.

***There were some little incidents that used to happen on ships. I remember one particular ship, a Swedish ship it was, oh, many years ago. We used to trade between Scandinavia and north west Africa and Preston UK. The ship's chandler happened to be a woman in her fifties, I think – anyway, she and the captain had a little thing going – she delivered the stores down to the ship, and he used to pay her in more ways than just currency. He was also married in Sweden, and I met his family and wife as the Swedish and Scandinavians were more friendly than most British captains. You would not get a British captain saying to you, "Come up to my cabin Eddy and meet my family," but the Scandinavians are more open.

This ship's chandler was down every night and she would leave in the morning. I used to say to the captain, "That ship's chandler was down early this morning captain." I would be up at 5.30am and see her going off the ship. He used to laugh and wave his fingers at me and I used to say to her, "Good morning you are early, I never saw you come on board this morning." "I forgot to put the clock back," she said laughing. I overheard her saying to the captain, "That young fella from Liverpool made a remark about not seeing me come on board." He said, "You mean Ted (that's me), oh, take no notice of him with his Liverpool wit," and started laughing. That was 50 years ago – doesn't time fly!

I forgot to mention the miners' strike in 1984. It was very bitter with the Tory government closing down the mines, which in turn destroyed communities and split families against each other. Our union RMT backed them fully. And also let us not forget the dock strike in Liverpool in 1995 – men with a proud heritage fighting for their jobs and the future for others coming through, good men all of them. I was proud, along with other union members, to go on the march with them and support them in their struggle. They can hold their heads up high and be proud of themselves. Another industry lost to an uncaring and ruthless Tory government at that time.

Resolution Bay

Act I

MV Boswell

Silversand - Iron Ore Ship

On way to Japan - Maersk Jupiter

Me and Motorman with Barracuda

Scottish Star
Gisborne, New Zealand

Pacific Blade, Towing Rig

Anvil Point

SS Roland

At Ascension Island 1988

SS Roland

Act I

Blue Funnel

Suez Canal

Australia Star 1979 - Maiden Voyage

M/V "Maersk Navarine" Panama Canal

Approaching St Lawrence Seaway

Iraqi Tanks from Gulf War
M/V Anvil Point

California Star

P.P. Container Ship

Maesk Nautilus - Panama Canal

Bay Boat En Route to Far East
Transit - Suez Canal 1995

Snow Storm

English Star

Churchill

Ceramic

MV Beechwood

Roland 1969

Store Room - Hurst Point

Suez Canal

Peninsular Bay, Japan 1995

Avelona Star - Port Stanley, Falklands 1984

The A. Holt & Co. cargo liner Menestheus, 8,510grt, built by the Caledon SB. & E. Co., Dundee, in 1958; she was renamed Onitsha in 1977 and was sold in 1978 to Greek buyers and renamed Elisland; she was broken up at Kaohsiung in 1979 (Picture: FotoFlite, New Romney)

Menestheus

Galley Girls - Hong Kong

Me and 2nd Cook - 1995

Dutch Marines

New Zealand 1974

Galley Girl - Hong Kong

Book Presentation
Odessa, Russia 1985

MV East Gate

Swan River

Ulster Star

Shell Tanker - Himea

Hobart Star

Persic

Ocean West

Jervis Bay

Across the Western Ocean

Hurst Point, St Lawrence Seaway, Canada

Relaxing, Hurst Point

Doughnuts for Smoko

Friends in Penang, Malaysia

BBQ Hurst Point

65th Birthday, at Sea, with cadet

Canada

40 Years Union Medal with John Tilly and Sam Brown

Tommy Keith, Peter Hall
and Gerry Dyson

With Joe Dobbs in London

Bar in Japan 1963 - Me in middle
with John Taylor and Griff

Maersk Jupiter - Singapore 1987

Blue Star Reunion with Neil McBride and Chris Mullaney

With Lee Petts

Reunion 2015 in Wales

Trevor, Teresa and Tyley

Jeff Rawlinson and Tony Proc

Vince Cowie

With Ricky Strike and The Lads

With Mick Brown
and Jimmy Derbyshire

Blue Star Flag Reunion

Barry Sinclair and Steve Warry

Moana from New Zealand

With Mick Brown

Chapter 6
Meeting Lenny Perry

O n my next trip I was to join the *Repulse Bay* in Southampton. July 1994. It was one of the new container ships *P&O* had added to their fleet. It had a crew of about 18, I think, and we sailed to the Far East. Out via the Suez Canal to Jeddah Saudi Arabia, Colombo Malaysia, Singapore, Hong Kong, Korea and Japan – about four ports there. As I said, the ships were very fast and we never spent much time in port. The round trip took around seven weeks.

I came home in September and a few weeks later I joined the *Liverpool Bay*. She was built in the 1970s but was ahead of her time. Lovely accommodation, all single berth, and a big galley to work in. Originally she was a steam ship when she first came out and was then converted to a motor vessel. Later on we sailed from Southampton to the Far East again and I came home at the end of November.

A few weeks later I was appointed to the *Tokyo Bay*, a ship of the same class as the *Liverpool Bay*, going out to the Far East again arriving home in February 1995. I spent Christmas at home. You used to get all the Chinese shops come on board selling various things – paintings, clothes, ornaments. They would come down, measure you for a suit and you would pick it up on the way back homeward-bound. On my first trip to the Far East I bought for my mother a lovely 52-piece Japanese dinner set. It cost me about £5 then. We still have it over at my sister's to this day.

A Chinese lady would come on board then. It was customary for her to cook for all the shop staff as well as the crew. It would give us cooks a break, so we could take a half-day off in Hong Kong.

She would clean down for us, we would give her a few bits and bobs to take home, and everyone was happy.

I joined the *Mairangi Bay* in March 1995 in Tilbury. This time we were to go to Australia and New Zealand via Cape Town South Africa, then back home and to Tilbury around Cape Horn, South America – a twelve-week trip. It was a fine big ship built about the late 1970s / early 1980s, I think. I had a very good second cook/baker with me on that trip, Ian his name, from around Aberdeen somewhere, on the east coast of Scotland. He was an ex-baker from the passenger ships, so I picked up some things from him on the bakery. You are never too old to learn. We had a good trip to Australia and New Zealand, and met up with a few friends I had known over the years. John Lamb came down to the ship in Adelaide and we went ashore for a few drinks. John was well retired but he used to like coming on board the ships.

I came home in June 1995 for a few weeks. I was to do my last trip with *P&O* containers as I had the offer of another job on a supply ship up in the North Sea. It was a big decision for me to make because I had been deep sea all my life, and to go and work in the North Sea, four weeks on four weeks off, was a big change. A big change in the weather too. This particular day I was home and I got a phone call from some bloke in Scotland. He said he was an operations manager for a catering company in Aberdeen that supplied cooks for the oil rigs and supply vessels that went out to them. Anyway, on with my story. He asked me if I had been in the *Blue Star Line* years ago. I said yes. He asked me was I the Eddie Bolton who sailed in the *Columbia Star* in 1972. I said yes and he asked me if I remembered him. He told me his name and I remembered he was the catering boy on the same ship. He told me he went to the oil rigs in the 1970s and had worked his way up to camp boss and ended up as operations manager. He asked me if I would be interested in a job on the supply boats. I told him I was working at the moment and was due to join a ship the next week. He said to give him a ring when I got home. He explained the conditions – four weeks on, four weeks off, full pay, and I must admit the salary was very good (as it was then on the rigs). I said I would think it over on my way home and call him.

I joined the *Kowloon Bay* in New Jersey USA so I flew out to New York from the UK. It was July 1995. The ship had gone on a new run – not the usual Southampton to the Far East – we were trading between the east coast and Gulf ports of the USA, then to the Far East via Jeddah and Colombo, also Malta on the way out. It was a good run and I enjoyed it. I had given some hard thought to going for the other job in the North Sea and decided to try it. I put in my resignation with *P&O* containers and I remember the captain saying to me, "Make sure you get the job first." I thanked him. Anyway, my mind was made up, I was leaving. I got home in October from Algeciras in Spain and I phoned the operations manager, Bob. He wanted me to go up to Invergordon to go on an oil rig for two weeks before I went on the supply ship. I was not that keen but thought I'll give it a try. He told me to get the train up to Aberdeen and he would meet me. So I got up there about at 8pm and he was there to meet me. He hadn't changed much. It had been 23 years since I had seen him, so we chatted over things and he said he would sort me out. After I had done the rig job he booked me a hotel. I got to Invergordon the next morning and went out to the rig by launch, as there were only about 25 on board. When they are on location, you can get up to 100 or 150 on a submersible.

The job I was doing was as night cook/baker. I met the chef, a lad from Newcastle, who helped me settle in. It was a big change from 'deep sea' and I was having doubts about whether I had made the right decision. Anyway, I picked up the job OK and came off after two weeks, got the train back down to Aberdeen and called in the office to see Bob. He said, "OK Eddie, go home and I will call you for the job on the supply ship in a few weeks." I said, "OK."

Before I got home in Aberdeen, I got talking to an old lady and she asked me what my job was. I told her I was a seaman, that I was a cook and that I had just been working on an oil rig temporarily until I got back on the ships. She told me that her son had been a cook at sea and that he had been killed. I asked her what happened and she asked me if I remembered a ship called the *Royston Grange*.

Then I knew what she was going to tell me. The *Royston Grange* was coming out of Buenos Aires in 1972 with a cargo of beef for the UK when she was in collision with an oil tanker. The *Royston Grange* caught fire and everyone on board perished, both crew and passengers, including some children. It was a big tragedy. I chatted to her and told her that I had been to Buenos Aires and had visited the seamen's mission *Stella Maris*. There has a memorial book with everyone's name in it who had died and I had been to a mass for them all. She was really happy that I had spoken to her and I told her that they will always be remembered there, and that they have a service every year for the victims. Anyway, she got off the train at the next station and I said goodbye and not to worry, and she thanked me for talking to her about it all.

As I got off the train in Aberdeen, another lady approached me and said, "I think you made an old lady very happy." She had heard what we were discussing. That was nice to think she went away after speaking about her son to me. Maybe she could not speak about it before, but with me being a seaman, it must have reminded her of her son.

As I said, after I went home I was waiting for Bob to call me about the job on the supply ships. A few weeks went by so I decided to call him. When I got through to reception I asked for Bob Mowvacs, the operations manager. To my great surprise I never expected the answer I got. He does not work here anymore. Well you can imagine how I felt. "Where is he?" I asked. "Don't know," they said. I told the receptionist that he had offered me a job and that I had left employment to come here. "I'm sorry," she said. So that was that! I was angry. I tried to contact him. I was even going up there to confront him, but to no avail – he had vanished. I told the union man in Aberdeen what he had done and he told me that he had done the same thing to other people. What did he get out of doing that? After all, the job situation was not that good, I'd had a run of bad luck for a time and was sorry that I had left *P&O* containers. I had never felt so bitter about anyone before, but I had to move on and you learn by your mistakes. A costly one at that.

I did get a job on a supply boat in December 1995. It was a ship belonging to *Farstad*, a Norwegian company with a British crew. I was there for two weeks over the Christmas period. The ship was doing coastguard duty in the English Channel. I came off at Dover and went up to Aberdeen to join the *Far Scotsman* for one week doing supply work to the rigs. The weather was atrocious. It was the North Sea.

I was home for three months until I got my next ship and I had just found out that *P&O* had made everyone redundant. The jobs were becoming harder to get now. I got a call in April 1996 to go and join a drill ship in Barcelona for two months. It belonged to *James Fisher and Sons* of Barrow. I got a flight out to Barcelona from Liverpool and joined the *Whitethorn*, a small drill ship which usually worked in the Mediterranean and West Africa but as it was, it was laid up in Spain waiting to be sold. It was an old coaster built in the 1950s I think, and later converted to a drill ship with a derrick and moon pool on deck. I was only feeding about ten people on board but when on location you could be feeding up to 40 or 50 people – drillers, surveyors and scientists – but I was on my own. It was a good job and the weather was getting hotter. Barcelona was a nice place, so I used to go ashore at night. It was a long walk but eventually I got a bike and cycled up to town, locked it up and walked around. There were a lot of nice bars and restaurants in town.

Whilst I was on the ship one morning I opened the galley door leading aft of the ship – the stern end. It was 5.30am as I was always up at that time. There was a cat there. Anyway, I gave it some milk and food and it went on its way. It started to visit me every morning and it was getting bigger. I thought it was all the tuna and salmon I was giving it – it must have been the best fed cat in Barcelona. It started to go into the store rooms and cupboards. I thought it strange, but for health and safety reasons I had to keep it out on deck – but it still kept coming for about ten days. Then one day when I opened the galley door there was no cat. Maybe it had gone ashore in the shed or something. I was a bit concerned for it, as with most seamen I like animals. Anyway

I thought no more about it until a week later one morning I opened the door and there was the cat walking up and down and looking a lot slimmer. It kept running around the side of the ship and back to me as if it was trying to tell me something. I followed it and it ran down the ladder to the drill deck. It kept looking back to see if I was following it. It went to the next deck down where all the tools were kept for the drills and engine room. Next thing the cat jumped into a box on the deck and then looked out for me. I came over and to my surprise there were about five kittens – not very old, only a few days I think. It was as if the cat was telling me to come and look at these kittens.

I went up and told the captain and the lads on the ship. He was surprised as well. Anyway, I fed the cat and then the next week it started carrying the kittens one by one up to the galley store room. I had to keep taking them down, then it would put them in another place. This went on every day. Eventually they started to get bigger and we found homes for them with people we had met in the cafés, bars and restaurants. My time was up, time to go home. I had been on the ship for seven weeks so the cook who relieved me looked after the cat when I went home. I came home in June, was home one week then got a job on a survey boat up in the North Sea, but I didn't like it. I was the night cook feeding about 30 people. I did six weeks there and came off in Yarmouth.

The next ship I went on was the *Amersham*, a container ship of about 6,000 tonnes, or near that. It belonged to an American company *Sealand* and it traded between Felixstowe where I joined it, to Portugal, Spain, Italy and Greece. A six week round trip. I joined it the end of October 1996. We went to the Mediterranean and back to the UK. We sailed again just before Christmas and spent Christmas Day in the Bay of Biscay. I tell you, the weather was horrendous, force 10 to 12, with the ship all over the place. How I did Christmas dinner I don't know. Even the lads said that. We lost a container, one was smashed open, and a lifeboat was damaged. We got into Lisbon on Boxing Day. It was one of the worst weather conditions I had ever been in. My cabin was right forward and the ships anchor had been banging against where my bed was. Was I glad to get into port! We got the damaged boat repaired, discharged the cargo and then on to Algeciras in Spain.

One of the seaman I met on there had been on the *Empress of Canada* with me in 1969. His name was Lenny Perry, a big man and a nice fella. He could drink! He could do a bottle of Four Bells rum a day and still do his job. The captain who was on this voyage was not the regular captain. Lenny used to call him Basil Rathbone, the film start who played Sherlock Holmes in the 1940s. He dressed the same and had a pipe in his mouth all the time. Anyway, on Christmas Day he would not give any beer out and said Lenny was drinking too much. I went along and said, "Captain, I need a bottle of rum for the Christmas pudding." "Ok," he said. "And Brandy for the sauce." "Ok," he said. I used what I wanted and gave the rest to Lenny! When we got to Pirreaus in Greece, the other captain came back on and when he was coming up the gangway Lenny brought his bag up for him. "How is the trip going Lenny?" "Oh not so good Captain," Lenny replied. "Why?" said the captain. "Basil Rathbone stopped my tap (beer ration)." "Who is Basil Rathbone?" he said. "This relief captain," said Lenny. "Come up to my cabin in an hour," he told Lenny. When the relief captain went ashore Lenny went up to see the captain who went down to the bond and gave Lenny a case of beer and a bottle of rum. He thought the world of Lenny, as he was an excellent seaman and saved the ship from hitting another ship when the mooring rope came away in Bilbao. It could have caused serious damage if not for Lenny's quick thinking. He was a great character, one of the last. I would say he is well retired now.

I came off the *Amersham* in Algeciras and flew home from Gibraltar in January 1997. The next ship I went on was an ex-*Esso* coastal tanker built in the 1960s now owned by *Everards*. I joined in Greys, Essex on the Thames and left three weeks later in Aberdeen. I was home a month and then I got a job on a survey ship called the *Charles Darwin*. I went for an interview in Southampton, got the job and joined the ship in Portugal on the 21 May 1997. We just stayed around the Spanish coast sailing up and down. I didn't like the job on there for some reason – wasn't that keen on the people on board – unusual for me. The chief steward was one of the reasons. I stayed for four weeks and came off in June in Southampton. I was home about five weeks and went up to Aberdeen on a standby boat that stays by the oil rigs in case of emergency. It was summertime and the weather was lovely. The job was so easy. Nobody had breakfast, a light lunch and dinner and a sweet at night – cold meats and salads. I was finished at 5.15pm. I did four weeks out in the Norwegian sector. That ship was called the *Hornbeck Castor*.

I got a job with the *Maersk* company again on one of their new anchor handlers that had just been built in Norway. I went out there to Norway in September and was on it for five weeks around Scotland and the west coast of Ireland moving oil rigs. It was when I got home I got a call from a company, *James Fishers* in Liverpool, to see if I wanted a job on one of the drill ships called the *Norskalld*, previously named *Pholas* and before that the *Elizabeth Bowater* belonging to *Bowaters* the paper ships. They used to go from Ellesmere Port to Canada with paper or for paper, I'm not sure. *James Fisher* converted it to a drill ship.

I decide not to go back to the *Maersk* beater, the anchor handler, as I was due to go down to Angola West Africa. I was not that keen on the captain so I joined the *Norskkald* in Ancona at the end of November. I had Christmas in Algeciras and sailed down to Abidjan on the Ivory Coast, then on to the Congo. I paid off in Abidjan and got home on the 26 January 1998. I was not staying on ships for long periods apart from that. A lot of changes were taking place in the industry.

The next ship I got a job on was a cable laying ship called the *Nexus*. It was managed by *James Fishers and Sons* of Barrow-in-Furness. I was to fly out to the ship which was at a place in Japan called Kitakyushu, on the south island of Kyushu. I had last been there on the *Lamport and Holt* ship, the *Roland*, when we got a Brazilian charter in 1969/70. I flew to Osaka then down to Fukuoka, spent the night in a hotel, then down to the ship the next day. Bob Banks was the day cook on there and I was the night cook as it was a 24-hour working ship. I began my shift at 7 in the evening and finished at 7 at night. It was a mixed crew of Philippine and British. The ship was laying cables between the islands. I spent seven weeks there and we got flown home for crew change. I only did this one trip there and I signed off in Moji. We did manage to get ashore a few times. I always liked going ashore in Japan, especially the Karaoke bars. You would get a laugh and then, of course, the girls.

I was home two months and then got a job on a ship called the *Global Mariner* an ex-*Bank Line* ship now run by the *ITF*. *ITF* is a big organisation that helps seafarers from all nations to get proper pay and conditions. Anyway, they managed this ship which was going to go around the world to hundreds of different ports highlighting safety aspects and inviting people to visit the ship on arrival in ports. Trips were three months on and three months off with two crews. I got a job on it as second cook as I thought it would be an interesting project. I joined the ship in Amsterdam I think or Rotterdam. Anyway, I only lasted 18 days. The captain was a good man, as were the mates.

What happened was when the ship got to Antwerp, everyone was ashore as usual after finishing work having a few beers. Anyway, there was another guy from Germany overseeing the project, an ex-captain. I think he was involved in Greenpeace as the story goes. When our captain and the mate came back from ashore, this man wanted to breathalyse them. I believe they had had a run in with him before over various things. They refused to blow into the bag and they got sacked. When some of the crew heard about it, we were not happy as he was a fair man. We went up to see him and asked if what we'd heard was right. He said yes and told us, "Don't do anything that will cost you your job." We told him that we did not think it was right about him and the second mate getting sacked. Anyway, they left through resignation, so when the ship got round to Lisbon I left the ship along with Peter Sam and AB from North Wales. The ship was not happy and not run properly. Not only that, there were also seamen on the ship who were there just for the money and the time off. They were not interested in the union, and some had only worked on ferries and managed to get on the *Global Mariner*. I believe it did finish its round the world trip and ended up sinking in the Orinoco River in South America.

A week later I went on a standby ship called *Viking Viper* for four weeks out in the North Sea off Yarmouth in October. The weather was atrocious – it was hard to cook in bad weather but you get used to it. Big ships or small ships, it's the same in bad weather. I came off in Yarmouth. I had two months home and I got a call for a job on an anchor handler vessel. I joined it in Flushing Holland in February 1999. The ship was small and had about 35 people on board as it was doing ROV work and had scientists and technicians on board. The normal complement was a crew of twelve, so here I was feeding 35 people. It was hard going and I asked one of the ABs why they had not got an extra cook on board for night work. He told me that the cook who was on leave said he could manage without another cook on because he was getting double pay, which was all wrong. He should have got another man. I asked the captain and he said the company would not give me any help. I did four weeks and I was tired when I got off. I was well paid but would sooner have had another man. The ship was working in the English Channel and I came off in Dover and went home. The captain and crew were all good. Bernie Nearny AB from Manchester was a great help to me in the galley and the mess-rooms and was a character as well.

Another friend of mine, Tony Lloyd (a cook from Manchester), called me to see if I was interested in a job as a cook on a new ferry service starting up from Folkestone. I said yes and he told me they needed a steward and did I know anyone? So I told Sam Brown and Tosh, two friends of mine, and we all got a start on the ferry. It was a few years old and had been working up the Baltic, and *Falcon Freight* had chartered it for the Folkestone Boulogne run. The ship was called *Neptunia*. It was a good job. We had two Portuguese cooks, one was good, the other not so. He was on nights and he made the custard and put salt instead of sugar in it and blamed someone else! I was on there for four weeks and then I got a job on a survey ship called the *Oceanic Cavalier*. I went out to Gibraltar dry dock to join her in May. In Gibraltar it was sold to *James Fisher's* and was renamed *Fisher's Cavalier*. I remained on her for four weeks then came home. A few weeks later I was back on a standby ship out in Liverpool Bay for four weeks on a ship called *Sefton Supporter*, managed by *Gulf Offshore*. It was summertime – June/July – and a good little job and plenty of nice weather. What more could you ask for?

I was longing to go back to deep sea but there was not a lot of jobs in that sector and they were hard to get. When I came off the standby boat I went across to Dublin by ship and down to Rosslaire to do a few weeks work on the *P&O* ferries European pathfinder running between Ireland and Cherbourg. I came back to Liverpool via Dublin. I was getting work on a regular basis and in August got a job on a dredger called the *Sand Siren* with *South Coast Shipping*. It was a good little job feeding eight crew and I joined it in Yarmouth by launch, going over to France and south coast English ports. Me and the captain would go ashore and buy the stores – all good food, pastries and bread – in France, and all the meat and vegetables in the UK. We fed well. I paid off four weeks later in Belgium and got the ferry home and the original cook went back. No wonder, it was a cushy little job.

I was home three weeks and got a call from *Gulf Offshore* in Aberdeen – would I be interested in a job on a supply boat. I said yes and went up to Peterhead, stayed in a hotel overnight and joined the ship the next day. The ship was quite new, and painted green – it belonged to *Sanko Line* but was managed by *Gulf Offshore*. It was mid-October, with winter coming up in the North Sea. We were running out of the port of Peterhead to the Forties Field Far North and no time in port, just constant port to oil rigs. And the weather – well the ship was all over the place for three weeks. I was on her as cook and came back early. Was I glad! I was still trying to get my balance walking in Aberdeen airport for my flight home. It was very hard trying to cook. One time it was so bad that oil came out of the fryers, so it was a good job I had them switched off. I had not slept properly for three weeks with the rolling of the boat.

After a few weeks home I got a job on a dredger. The company was *Hanson Aggregates* and I was on there for six weeks, three weeks on and three off. As I said earlier, the jobs for deep sea were not coming up so you had to take what was around. I was getting my work from the agency. My next job was on a standby boat belonging to *North Sea Shipping* Aberdeen, so I was back up the North Sea again, but it was not so bad as it was in summertime. I did four weeks on the ship and a month later I got a job on a ship called the *Ernest Shackleton*, a research vessel owned by the *British Antarctic Survey*. This ship usually goes down to the Antarctic for six months just after the British summer but when I joined the ship as chief cook it was doing survey work in the North Sea. The catering team was a chief steward, chief cook, second cook and also I think three stewards. We were kept busy as we had 60 to 70 personnel on board so we were cooking night and day.

The ship was really good – accommodation, galley and mess-rooms, dining room – one of the best set ups I have seen on a ship. A choice of three or four main courses lunch and dinner, a salad bar, cold cuts and fish, and the quality of the meat and stores was absolutely first class. The second cook, Simon was on nights – a good lad, and he had a steward working with him. The stewards were from Grimsby and good lads to work with and go ashore with when we were in port. However, the chief steward was starting to interfere with the galley and they don't usually do that. If the job is running ok they stay out. He was getting on all our nerves. One time I came on days and he was in his cook's clothes. He had been working all night with the second cook who also did not want him around. He was the chief cook before I arrived and he had got the chief steward's job. Anyway, I did not want to go away for six months down the Antarctic with him. As far as I am concerned only one man runs the galley and that's the chef. I went up to the captain and told him I was leaving and handed in my notice. He had an idea what was going on and he did not want me to leave because everyone was happy with the food – very much so. It was a big decision to make as I had always wanted to go to the Antarctic. I had never been there before and now I had lost the chance, but it was a blessing in disguise I suppose – as I tell you why.

The year before in 2001 I was having problems passing water from my bladder and had been going up to the Dreadnought Hospital in London for check-ups. I was diagnosed with an enlarged prostate, as it does when you get older. I was about 53 years of age so was getting regular check-ups in London. Not long after leaving the *Ernest Shackleton* I got a job on the *Swires* offshore anchor handler in Aberdeen. How I got the job was I was in the Crown and Anchor pub on the dock road in Aberdeen with my mates off the survey ship where I met the captain off the *Pacific Banner* who I had sailed with previously. He told me that the captain on the *Pacific Blade* needed a cook. I told him I was leaving the survey boat and he phoned up the personnel officer Christine Wain. She phoned me to say that I had got the job. Anyway, a week later I went up to Aberdeen again and joined it. I was in the process of moving house so when I came home after four weeks I moved to a one-bedroom flat in Alexandra Drive, Aigburth. I liked the *Pacific Blade* and the captain and crew were really good. There were only twelve of us on board so I was able to give them an à la carte menu with 36 choices at lunchtime.

It was during another trip to the hospital that I was to have a biopsy on my prostate. I came home a week later and went up to join the *Pacific Blade* in Aberdeen. We were just leaving the port when I was in the galley and my mobile phone went off. I answered it and it was Irene Boncelli, the lady who ran the administration for the Dreadnought who along with her colleagues do a splendid job for seamen. "Eddie," she said, "the consultant at Guys and St Thomas's hospital has called." I said to her that I was on a ship just sailing out of port. "I can't see him as I am on the ship for four weeks before I get off." She said, "It can't wait, you have to see him as soon as possible." So a week later I got off the ship and went home, then proceeded down to the hospital.

Let me explain this first about the Dreadnought. One time seamen had their own hospital in Greenwich called 'Dreadnought' but owing to government cutbacks they closed it down and allocated a number of wards for the treatment of seafarers and their dependents. It was funded by the government, so many millions of pounds to go to the Dreadnought facility. Anyway somewhere between the 1990s and 2000 we lost the wards that were allocated for seafarers, but now you still come under Dreadnought in Guys or St Thomas's hospitals according to your illness. They are still funded by the government to treat seafarers as quickly as they can.

It was in St Thomas's Hospital just opposite the Houses of Parliament that I had to go and see the consultant, Mr Tiptaft. The nurse came out and told me to go in to see him. When I got in the room he was sitting there reading my notes. I sat down and watched him, his eyes up and down the paperwork. It seems strange but I knew what he was going to say to me even before I came down on the train. Next thing he put down the papers and looked over to me. "Mr Bolton," he said, "we found a tumour on the prostate." So I said to him, "What is the next move then?" I was not nervous or even bothered. It was just like I was on one of my previous visits to see him. He then said, "We will have to operate. There are two ways, either radiotherapy – that means going down the urethra like a laser – or we may have to do a prostatectomy." He explained this was when they remove the prostate capsule altogether by surgical means, cutting open below my stomach. I asked him if it was a big operation and he said yes. I said to him, "How long will it be before I can go back to sea?" He said about six months and that he was putting me under another consultant, Mr O'Brien, who would be operating on me. He said I have booked an appointment with him for you. I said goodbye and thanked him for everything and went back to Liverpool on the train. To be honest it wasn't worrying me one bit, and that's the truth, I just carried on as normal, I even did another trip on the *Pacific Blade*. I told Norman the captain and the lads that I was going for an operation and got off the ship and there at home was a letter from Mr O'Brien the consultant.

I went down to the hospital and they kept me in for three days routine check-up pre-operation I think. Anyway, when the consultant came around with the doctors on his morning visit to the ward he came over to me and introduced himself. A man of about 40 years, very polite, he said to me, "You know what you are here for?" I said, "Yes I do." I had just finished the morning paper. He then said, "You can go home now and we will give you a date for the operation." So I got dressed and went back home. Jimmy Duggen, a retired seaman, had come in to see me because he lived in London – he was a really nice man who did a lot for seamen in hospital. I told him the script and what was happening and he said he would meet me when I got off the train.

I think being told you have cancer, to other people, must be a frightening thing. Some people can handle it better than others. I think I was one of those who could. Death does not frighten me, it comes to us all. My saying about death is that you don't remember coming into the world, so you won't remember going out of this world. Jimmy Duggan says every day is a blessing. I seem to worry about little things like, for instance, if I let somebody down or like if I have been home from sea and not visited people I know, when I should have. Yet being diagnosed with cancer I just carried on. But I think somebody was guiding me through. I think of my mother. She never feared death but worried over trivial things. And of course God – I believe there is someone up there.

The time came around for me to go down for my operation. It was October 2002. Jimmy Duggan met me at the station and we went across on the underground to the hospital. I booked myself in, got myself settled down in the ward and Jimmy went off and said he would return the next day. I had all the tests and in a few days was to have the prostatectomy. It was a big operation, an incision of about five inches I think. I had a good sleep the first night and the next morning got up around the ward. The hospital was excellent. The staff, nurses and doctors the same. It makes you realise how lucky we are to live in this country of ours and get this first class treatment free. Jimmy came in with the papers and fruit – he always came in with something he did – a very good man.

The next day I was going down for my operation. Mr O'Brien came around that morning and told me I was going to the operating theatre at about 10 o'clock next morning, so that night I had nothing to eat. I woke up in the morning, had a bath and put on the gown for going down to the theatre. The hospital porter came for me. As I had seen the anaesthetist the previous evening who told me what was happening, I got down to the theatre and someone gave me an epidural needle in the spine and another one to put me out.

The next thing I remember was waking up in the recovery ward at about 7 o'clock at night, I think it was. I had a lot of tubes in me and Mr O'Brien said I had lost a lot of blood, so I was having blood put into me. I felt really hungry anyway. Jimmy Duggan had left a bowl of fruit in the ward for me so I ate some grapes. I also had a catheter in me to release my urine into a bag. I had a sleep and woke up in the morning for medication and painkillers. I had some toast and tea but felt a bit weak. The third day the nurse had me out of the bed to try and walk, but I was so weak I could not stand. The fourth day I was ok. I had a visit from Jimmy Duggan, Mark Wong and John Pattersson (who has passed away since, a lovely man). They had been staying in Springbox, a convalescent home for seamen. The next day my cousin from Watford came in with his wife and his daughter Vicky. Also a mate of mine off the ship I was on before came up from Liverpool. Nick was a second mate but is a captain now. I had plenty of phone calls from family and friends, and my aunts Margaret in America and Doreen in Devon. The priest came to see me as well.

Mr O'Brien came in on the Sunday morning to check on me. The weather outside was very bad. He said I bet you wouldn't like to be at sea now. He told me I could go home in a few days and that I should come back in a few weeks to have the catheter taken out. After a week in hospital I got up and waited for Jimmy Duggan to come and take me across to Euston station on the tube. I said thank you and goodbye to everyone and we went across to Euston. I was still feeling weak and still had the catheter in me, making it difficult to walk. I got to Euston, got on the Liverpool train, thanked Jimmy and told him I would see him again in about a fortnight when I went down to get the catheter out.

I arrived in Liverpool and my friend Derek Creed came in the car and took me home to my flat in Alexandra Drive and then we went for something to eat. I had to keep emptying the catheter as the bag was filling up with water. I just relaxed at home for a week and then went out on the bus to town. After a fortnight home I went back down to Guy's Hospital to get the catheter out. Jimmy was there again to take me across on the tube. I had lost a bit of weight but was getting better slowly.

I still had to go down to the hospital a few times. I had the operation in October and I was back at sea in March 2003. I joined an anchor handler out in Malabo in Equatorial Guinea, West Africa. I was there for six weeks and flew home to the UK via Switzerland. That ship was owned by *Swires Pacific*, the company I was with before. I never went back. I had a bit of leave and I got a job a few weeks later on a supply boat belonging to *Gulf Offshore*. She was doing ROV work, trenching the ocean so that they could lay telephone cable. I joined in Aberdeen and we left doing the job on our way to the Faroe Islands. It took us four weeks to do the job, the first time I had ever been there – it was a nice, quaint place. We arrived back in Scrabster, the top of Scotland where I paid off. I was night cook/baker and a lad named Joe, a Scottish lad from Northampton, was the day cook. He was a nice lad, I got on with him. The ship was the *Highland Eagle*. I was starting to have a bit of trouble below so I had to go back down to hospital in London.

They kept me in for a few days and did some investigations, then took me down to the theatre. I was in there three days and the morning I was to go home the nurse told me to drink plenty of water, which I did. Anyway, I could not pass water and I was in agony. The doctors came and put an incision in my groin and put in a catheter. What a relief! I then had to go back to theatre again as some skin inside the bladder was blocking my urethra so I could not pass water. Anyway, next day I went on my way. I thought to myself I would call in to my relations. I went to the supermarket to buy some food and I needed to go to the toilet. The next thing was I could not pass water again, so I went to the hospital in Watford. I was in agony again! I felt as if I would burst my bladder. Anyway they took me in emergency and I had another catheter fitted to enable me to pass water. I went back to my Aunt Kathleen's house and rang the hospital In London and told them what had happened.

They told me to get back down the next day, so I went off back down to London. They kept me in a day and it was another blockage. The next day I had the catheter off and went straight back to Liverpool.

That evening everything was fine, but the next morning when I got up I could not pass water again, so I had to take a taxi to the hospital in Liverpool where they attended to me. I had to go back to the hospital in London. Again everything seemed to get better and I had to learn how to put a catheter in me in case I ever could not pass water. This I was able to do and I was ok after a few times. I still had to go down to the hospital in London for regular check-ups every three months. The whole staff team of nurses and doctors in London was marvellous and dedicated to their job. They got to know me well the times I went down there. I was becoming part of the furniture, the nurses used to joke.

A couple of weeks later I was back on ship, a dredger called *The Dolphin*. It was summertime and the job was temporary, which suited me at the time. I was there three weeks when a friend, Darrell Ireland (and also a cook), phone saying that there was a cook's job going on one of the *Bibby* ships chartered to the MOD. Was I interested? So I rang them and three days later I was on my way to Southampton to join the ship. It was a big one, 20,000 tonnes I think, and not very old. A big roll on roll off ship which could carry military vehicles, tanks, lorries, ammunition and containers. It was going down to the Falklands Islands to the military base down there. The trip would be about eight weeks. The voyage on the way down was in good weather, but after leaving the Ascension Islands a week later, the weather was really bad for about five days. I really thought the ship was going to go over and it was that bad that the galley and the store-rooms all came away. It was like a bomb had hit it. It was not until we got down to the Falklands that we were able to clean up the mess. Everyone helped us – Sean Flynn, the bosun from Middlesbrough, and Joe Nicks, the second cook, and all the lads. The voyage on the way back was a lot better after passing the Ascension Islands then up towards the African coast. It was really hot. When the ship called at the Ascension Islands the lads went fishing and came back with about 15 big tuna which we were eating every day as an extra entrée! It was lovely. We finally arrived in Marchwood across from Southampton where I left the ship and went home. It was October. The ship was called the *Hartland Point* and the captain was Angus McPherson. He told me he served his time as a cadet in the *Bank Line*. I was to sail with him again later.

These ships were fine, big ships, with nice single berth accommodation with toilet and shower. Of a night time after work we would all socialise with darts games, cards, horse racing meetings and we would put on a snack. There are big changes today at sea. The crews are a lot smaller and of a night time it is quiet, as a lot of the crew are keeping watch. Some of the lads have a few beers on the bar. You have to be careful of the amount you drink now as someone is likely to come down and breathalyse you. Years ago that never happened.

I was home for four months as I had to go back for check-ups on my health and make sure everything was ok to go back to sea. I got a call from Nicky Davenport, personnel manager for crewing the ships, asking me would I fly out to join the *Anvil Point* in Fujarah in the Persian Gulf. We went to Iraq, the port of Umm Quassar and then proceeded to Muscat in Oman. We had twelve soldiers on board for security against attack by pirates and also to check the tanks and armoured vehicles were ok on passage. After Muscat we went down to the Red Sea and then picked up the pilot at Port Tewfik, Suez and then proceeded through the Suez Canal and on to Limmasol in Cyprus where I got off and came home.

Chapter 7
Union

Due to the decline in the merchant navy we don't get a big attendance like the old days – we just don't have the members. As I said, we used to be called the National Union of Seamen, then we went with the rail union and became the RMT – the Rail, Marine and Transport Union. After we had our BGM meeting in Portsmouth I went to join the *Anvil Point* in Marchwood. The ship was going on a NATO exercise to the east coast of the USA so we loaded all military equipment – French, Dutch and British vehicles, along with eight French marines and two Dutch marines. They were on board to look after the transports on the crossing to our first port, a place called Moorehead City in North Carolina, where everything went off and headed to the marine camp out in the country somewhere. There were a lot of Royal Fleet Auxiliary and Royal Navy ships there.

We were there for a few weeks and it was a nice little town. We also went to Norfolk Virginia, then back to Moorehead City to load the vehicles and transports, and then we continued our journey back to France and Holland to discharge our cargo and marines. It was a nice little trip – two months.

Whilst I was home I went to the RMT Biennial General Meeting that was held in Portsmouth where we could discuss things on the agenda to make sure everything was going ok, and bring up some points that needed addressing. You get to meet a lot of people from the shipping grades. Bob Crow, our then leader, was there, as well as Steve Todd and Peter Hall. Mick McQuaid from Belfast was there with his lovely wife, John Moran with Joan from Liverpool, and Jimmy Duggan came down from London as an observer (he was retired then still active). I believe that all union members should try and get to their branch meetings. It is very important. We don't always agree with some things, we have our ups and downs, but that is what it is all about. Voice your opinions and we, the members, are the union. The union officers in the Liverpool branch, Andy Boyak and John Tilley, are all very good and will help you with everything you need. Sam Brown, the branch secretary is very good. He works offshore on the oil rigs in Liverpool Bay and he always lets us know when there is a branch meeting by text on the mobile phone – all this modern technology eh?!

A few days later I flew out to Port Stanley from Brize Norton to join the *Anvil Point*. The cook, Ian Simpson, had to go home as his mother had died. It was a long flight to the Falklands, first stopping off at the Ascension Islands, then on to Stanley. I arrived on the ship at 5 o'clock in the evening and Angus McPherson was the captain and Carl Power the second cook. We sailed and got back to Southampton where I paid off. Before I went on the *Anvil Point* I had a job for three weeks on a *BP* coastal tanker. I joined it in Aberdeen. The captain wanted me to do a watch and I would not do it. You sign on as AB/cook, but they never told me that and they also required me to let go and tie up. The old man was a nice guy and said he would train me up, but I declined. I left in Grangemouth Scotland.

A few weeks later I got a job on a dredger owned by *RMC Marine*. It was called the *Sand Harrier*. I went over to Le Havre to join it and I did not like it at all. You had to go to the supermarket for the food, but I never got enough money to buy the stores. I came down to start work one morning and when I got in the galley the sink was full of dishes. I left it clean and I expected it to be the same when I came down in the morning. I told the old man I was not happy with it and he was not interested, so I put my notice in and got off in a place called Cliff on the River Thames.

A few weeks later I was on another dredger working off the Norfolk coast and bringing sand to various ports on the Thames. The ship was the *Arco Arun*. Billy Flynn from Bootle was the other cook I relieved. He was in *P&O* Containers when I was there. The next ship I joined was the *RoRo Hartland Point* – I was to join it in

Port Said, Egypt. When I flew out to Cairo I was met in the airport by a driver to take me to Port Said which was a few hours drive away. He said he was to take me to a hotel in Port Said so I followed him to the car. There was another man who got into the car beside him. "Who is this man?" I asked the driver. He said, "Don't worry, he is with me." I was concerned what with all the kidnapping going on, and especially with me going to a ship that is taking military equipment to and from the UK to the Middle East. When I came back to put my bags in the back of the car, I made sure that I had my small bag with my cook's knives in near my side. I thought to myself if anything went wrong with these two individuals or if they tried anything, I would not go down without a struggle – that's for sure!

However, I jumped in the back of the car and we set off down the road. We stopped for coffee a few hours later, then moved on again. We were approaching a toll gate and the car slowed down. Two soldiers came to the driver and looked into the car. The driver and his friend pulled out ID cards and showed them to the soldiers. They waved us through no bother and the driver and his friend started laughing to themselves. Anyway, we soon arrived at the hotel in Port Said and the driver helped me in with my luggage. After that he said to me not to go outside the hotel until they came for me in the morning, and then he left. Maybe they were military themselves, or police, I don't know, but they had the guards on the toll gate moving us through fast.

I got up in the morning, had breakfast and then at about 2pm I was taken to clear immigration and then driven down to the Suez Canal where the ship *Hartland Point* was steaming towards us *en route* to the Mediterranean Sea, bound for Cyprus, Gibraltar and Marchwood. I went out in a small boat and went alongside the ship where I climbed the gangway, helped on board by the bosun. The other cook, Phil Lane, was going down the gangway. I settled in and the next day I turned in to the galley. The second cook was Hollywood, a bit of a bullshitter but harmless – he was ok. The weather was not too bad for November in the Med and we arrived back in Marchwood three weeks later where I came off. Later I was on my way to Port Said again to join the *Hurst Point* outside the Suez Canal, this time going to Iraq and Karachi. I went out in a launch again and got on board the ship. Joe Brown was the bosun, and the captain's name was Mike-Farmer.

I relieved Dominic the cook. He said he was glad to get off. I don't think he got on with the second cook, John Allenby. John was ok, I knew him from way back when he was younger, and he did like a drink! It was the 21st December, so I had a lot of work on to prepare for the Christmas dinner. Eventually I got it all done and when Christmas Day was over and I was able to relax. After the lads help us clean up – as they do at Christmas – we have a lot of DVDs on board and library books and a bar. I used to watch a movie or read a book then turn in as I was usually up at 5.30am.

The weather was warming up once we got into the Red Sea, then on to the Persian Gulf to Dubai, and Umm Qasr in Iraq, then to Karachi to discharge the cargo bound for Afghanistan where there was a lot of security around the ship. We had army personnel on board at all times when we were in the Middle East. After discharge we went back to Fujairah where I and John Allenby and the captain paid off, along with Brian Rowland an AB, and Carl Power relieved John as second cook. We went off in a launch and stayed in a nice hotel and flew back to the UK the next night via Amsterdam and Manchester. That was January 2006.

I was home three months this time and *Bibby's* had no work for me, but I got a call in April from one of the agencies to go and join a dredger in Middlesbrough on Teesside. The last time I was here was in 1975 when I joined the *Avelona Star* in Smith's Dock. How it had changed since then. It was like a ghost yard. Gone were the local workers it had when the shipyard was busy. All that was in the dry docks was the ship I was joining, the *Arco Adur*, and believe it or not all the shipyard workers were from Poland, not local labour. They used to fly them over from Poland if there were ships needing repairs. Mind you, they stopped training young lads for the ship repair industries and they now get the ships built abroad. To think we used to lead the world in shipbuilding. How times have changed. Anyway, I was on there for three weeks in dry dock. We used to go up to the supermarkets for our food stores, which wasn't far, and there were only about 15 of us on board. I left it and went home to Liverpool.

About a week later I joined another dredger belonging to *Westminster Dredging*. I joined her in Harwich. *The Medway* was the name of the ship. I was on there for about a week on relief duties. Dave Holbrook was the motorman on there – he used to be an AB but now I believe he is skipper on a small boat. I sailed with Dave in *P&O* containers. His twin brother Robert is a cook on the North Sea. We keep in touch on the laptop, which I am learning slowly. I came off in Harwich and caught the train home. I must say I have never seen a ship so well stored up and with a high feeding rate.

I got a ship with *Scottish Fisheries* on a ship called the *Mina*, a small boat with about 17 crew I think. Its purpose was to check the fish quotas the trawlers are catching. I joined her in Greenock on the tail of the Clyde and we were working up by the Shetland Isles and the North Sea. We used to get a lot of fresh fish, prawns and seafood. There was a good crowd of people on board. I was on her for three weeks. I could have had a permanent job on there but I prefer to move around different ships. I came off ship in Leith. Home another week and I got a call from *Gulf Offshore* to join one of their supply ships. I had to go to Den Helder in Holland. We were just taking supplies out to the rigs off Holland and I was on the ship for ten days. The airline lost my luggage and it was two days before I got it back. Good job the ship was still in port! The captain phoned the airline and said, "Get the luggage down, I'm waiting to sail." His name was Faz, a good man from Bangladesh who was living in Ireland. The name of the ship was the *Highland Piper* – not very old. Those ships are ok in the summer, but up in the North Sea in winter they can be bad, rolling all over the place.

I was starting to get regular work which kept me ticking over. A few weeks later I joined a dredger, again called the *Sand Falcon*, in Dover. I was on it three weeks working off the South Coast, and I left in Amsterdam – that was September 2006. The next month I re-joined it in Grimsby. It was a good job. Same thing – you went to the supermarket for food but the captain used to bring the potatoes and vegetables and cheese down to the ship in a hired car. That's what a lot of companies do now – let you have cars to join or leave the vessel in the UK. They never did that years ago, it was rail warrants instead. You still get them today. I came off the ship in Yarmouth. One of the crew hired a car and dropped me off by Irlam and I got the train home. A long drive from Yarmouth!

A few weeks later on 26th October 2006, I had to go into hospital in London to have an operation on my bladder as it was causing me problems. Anyway, I was in for three days and when I came out I had to have a catheter in while everything was healing up. I went back to the hospital five weeks later to have the catheter removed and everything was ok. After that I joined the *Hurst Point* for a trip down to West Africa to pick up some French army vehicles in Libreville to bring back to La Rochelle, a port in the Bay of Biscay. It was only a five-week trip. We sailed in December so had Christmas on the way down. A nice run with no bad weather – we loaded the army transport on and had French marines to watch over the trucks and other stuff we had loaded on board. We had a day or two then we sailed for home.

After a few days out, it was about 3 o'clock when I went to go around to the fridges which were on the same level as the galley, leading out on to the open deck. Next thing I saw were two or three African men holding each other up. I thought they were stowaways right away. I went over to them, they were in a bit of a state and cold. Anyway, I put a warm coat on them, sat them down and phoned the bridge, and then gave them some hot drinks and food which they relished, not having eaten for a few days I presumed. The Chief Mate came down to the galley and tried talking to them but they only spoke French, so I got the French marines to come and speak to them. After a while we got them settled down and put them in a spare cabin which we had to lock. We didn't know who they were and with a lot of piracy around that area you had to take precautions. However, they were well looked after, coming out for food and a chat with the French marines. Mick Whelan the second cook gave them some clothes, as did a lot of other people. They managed to get on board up the side of the ship, so they said, but maybe they were hidden in one of the vehicles. The captain was Ian Bunning and when we arrived in La Rochelle they were taken off and went to a detention centre. Whether they got asylum or not, I don't know. I would hope to think so given the current situation in the country they came from the Congo. Anyway, we arrived back in Marchwood, back in the cold weather, in January 2007.

I was hoping to get another deep sea trip. It would be nice to get into some warm weather. I really do like the warm climate, it makes me feel good and I love to go out on deck with a book and a mug of tea, just watching the sea go by as the ship is moving along.

Well, I did not have to wait long. I got a call from Bibby's to go down to Marchwood to join the *Eddystone* which was going down to the Falkland Islands, taking supplies to the British Forces stationed there. The weather started to get nice after passing Gibraltar and we headed down into the calm blue waters of the South Atlantic, passing Las Palmas and down on to Ascension Islands where we stopped off to discharge some cars and stores. A lot of people on there are from St Helena. It's mostly volcanic rock there. They have a NAAFI club and there was also an American base. I was there when the Falklands War was going on and it was very busy then, with a lot of ships and warships. Now it was so quiet. When the ship anchors, they bring out pontoons to take off the cargo and some of the lads go out fishing for yellow tail tunas – they are massive and I was well stocked up with it for ages, putting it on the menu – can't beat it, and it's also nice in a barbecue, which we had on the way down. It takes just over three weeks to get there and a few days alongside and then back to Marchwood – about a seven week trip with good weather most of the time and being summertime in the Falklands was not too bad either. We got back to Marchwood on 8th May.

I was home for about two months as it went a bit quiet on the job situation. I got a job in July on another dredger I was on in 2003, one called the *Dolphin* – a good little job. The stores were already put on board as I was only relieving and not a big crew, about twelve maybe. Anyway, I had to go to Birmingham Airport to fly out to Waterford. The ship was doing some dredging in the

Channel and we had some scientists on board, as where the ship was dredging there was a Royal Navy wreck from 200 years ago in this channel. Apparently it had been sunk by the Irish, who fired a cannon from a fort ashore. After we finished that job we came back to Cardiff – a nice crossing as it was July. After three weeks I came off in Cardiff and caught the train to Liverpool.

I went on the *Anvil Point* a few weeks later, down to the Falklands, an eight week round trip, and after that went to join the *Hurst Point* again for a trip down to the Falklands again. We had Christmas at sea and got back to the UK in February 2008.

After a week at home, I went out about midday one day to visit some friends. After seeing them I went to the bus stop and as I turned around the bus was coming so I started to run to the bus stop. I tripped, my foot catching in a hole in the pavement. I tried to miss the hole and the next minute I was on the pavement in agony. Luckily someone was on the other side of the road and he rang an ambulance. They came and looked at me and confirmed I might have fractured the femur on my left leg. When I got to the hospital they said I had fractured it. I was in for a week before I came home on crutches.

I was off work for six months, hobbling along on crutches and having physiotherapy. I was fit by July and I joined the *Hurst Point* again for a trip down to the Falklands – a nice little run down and back to Emdem in Germany, then back to the UK. Before I had joined the *Hurst Point* after my accident, I went off to Thailand for a three-week holiday in Phuket. I was still on my crutches but I still enjoyed sitting on the beach under the umbrella reading a book. There is always someone selling ice cream, cold drinks and food on the beach – really good.

It was December now and I got a job on a drill ship. The company was *Gulf Offshore* who I had worked with before. Anyway, I joined it in Falmouth on 16th December and sailed down to Angola. It was a smooth passage to West Africa, even the Bay of Biscay was calm for December. We had Christmas dinner on the way down. There were two cooks, Dave Idale from Liverpool and myself, and a steward from Belfast (I can't think of his name).

Once we got on location I went on nights as the ship was working 24 hours. We had about 50-odd on board, counting the drillers and contractors, so I was cooking for about 20 people. It wasn't too bad and we were not in bad weather, which made it easy. I came off the ship in Pointe Noire and flew home to Manchester Airport via France, then got the train up to Liverpool. I was only away five weeks.

Then ten days later I joined the *Hurst Point* in Glenmallon and went across the Atlantic to Three Rivers and Montreal Canada. It was January and the crossing was a bit rough. Once we got to the St Lawrence River it was all ice. It is a lovely sight on both sides of the river and the views are lovely. You see an awful lot of churches. I noticed they were built by French settlers and the Irish, so I'm told. Anyway that was only a short trip and I left the ship in Montreal and flew home. The cook came back early – after all I was only the relief cook and that suited me. I was home for a few months probably for hospital appointments as I had to keep an eye on things.

I started to go out to the Far East a lot to visit friends – to the Philippines where I met Gina in 1998 and visited her often, about once a year depending if she was working abroad in the Middle East on a long contract. I used to like to go to Cebu, one island of the many, and I also liked to go to Subic Bay which used to be a US naval base.

I also used to go to Penang in Malaysia. I stayed in the Mariners' Centre at a good price and the people that run it are good friends of mine. It has a couple of rooms and is used for crew changes off the ships – before and leaving the ship they stay the night here. The Mariners' Centre is situated in town and the ferry terminal is across the road, and you can go to Indonesia or Lankawi from there, and there is also a cruise ship terminal. You can also go across to the mainland to Butterworth, or anywhere really. It's an ideal location, and a few hours' drive to the Thai border, once you are over to the mainland.

They also have a large bridge across to the mainland and are building another to ease traffic congestion, which can be real gridlock in Penang with so many cars there. It really is a nightmare and you can spend hours in traffic as Penang is only an island. They are looking to build a rail system like they have in Singapore. When I'm there, I like to travel around Malaysia by bus. There is such lovely scenery to look at, stopping at motorway cafes for food and drink. Malaysia is one of the best places for variation of food – Indian, Malay and Chinese – and not expensive either. The hawker stalls are open well into the night.

I used to like to go over to Lankawi Island on the boat. It's about a four hour run, and it is nice and quiet there with plenty of duty free shops. I used to buy sweets and candy for my friends in the Mariners' Centre. They love them, especially *Cadbury's* chocolate. You have to make sure you get into the air-conditioned building before it melts. I have always liked the Far East, going back to when I was a boy sailing on the 'China boats', as the *Blue Funnel* ships were known then.

Once I decided to take the bus from Penang to Singapore, a journey of about 12 hours, and when I arrived at Johore Malaysia I went through immigration and customs. It was all ok until I got to Singapore customs. I had 200 cigarettes I bought in Malaysia and because I did not declare them, they told me I had to pay a fine of £1,000 or go to jail! I told them that you are allowed 200 cigarettes anywhere in the world you go, but they would not have it, so I had to pay the money. I was not happy about it – I don't even smoke! They were for one of the old seamen I knew in Liverpool, Gerry Dyson. They are very strict in Singapore. Some of the laws I agree with, but I thought that was a bit much. When I got home I wrote a letter to them expressing my views that I thought the fine was too much. The funny thing about it was that I had a Chinese meat cleaver and several sharp knives which I purchased in Malaysia for my work in the galley. They never said a thing about them being in my bag. The customs wrote back to me to say that I was very lucky not to get a jail sentence. What can you do?

About October time I joined the Hartland Point in Marchwood and we sailed to Norway, Germany, Montreal and a place called Beconcor on the St Lawrence River, opposite Three Rivers on the other side of the river. After Canada we proceeded down to North Carolina in the USA to load some military stuff. It was very hard to get shore leave considering we are their allies, and they made it hard for us to get ashore. As soon as the vessel arrived in the USA ports you had to report to immigration to get your name taken, and if you were lucky enough, to get a shore leave pass. Then you had the customs and agriculture inspectors come on board to check the fridges and storerooms to make sure everything was ok. Sometimes they sealed your fridges up if you had provisions not from the States. After you sailed, you could open and use them. The run down to Galveston from North Carolina was cold considering we were passing the Florida coast. The weather was bad and when we got to Galveston there was snow, believe it or not – very cold, and unusual for the Mexican Gulf. It's usually warm. We had a few days there to load a helicopter for the RAF who were training in the States for flying them in the Middle East theatre of war. After finishing cargo, we sailed for the UK, again with no shore leave, calling at Glenmallon, Scotland, then down to Marchwood. It was 4th January 2010.

We then went to Harstad in Norway to pick up military equipment to take back to the UK as the marines had been doing their winter training there. We arrived back in Marchwood and loaded for the Middle East. I got off the ship in Limassol Cyprus on 28th January and went home. I was home two months and then got a job on the *Hartland Point*. I have been on that a few times, and all the accommodation and galleys are the same as the other ships. We sailed to the continent and then down to Gibraltar calling at Crete, a lovely island. That's the first time I have been there and the weather was lovely. It was March so the Mediterranean was starting to warm up. After a few hours there on to Limassol, then through the Suez Canal to Aqaba in Jordan, then to Jebel Ali, Emirates, and on to Karachi, Pakistan, taking military stuff for Afghanistan. No one allowed to go ashore there. I would not fancy it anyway! It was really hot there, and we had the usual military personnel on board in case of pirates or terrorists. After leaving Karachi we went to Muscat in Oman, back to Aqaba, then back through the Suez Canal to Cyprus, and then Marchwood. I came off the ship there and was home for a while.

I got a call from an agency to go on a standby boat. It was multi-purpose standby and supply. The ship was called *Ocean Spey*. Their job is to go out to the oil rigs in case of an emergency operation on the rig. They are there to pick up survivors should one happen. This one was not so old, owned by a Norwegian company. I went up to Aberdeen to join it and the same day we were out to the rig. I've been on this kind of ship before but I was really sea sick for a day. I've been on other ships up in the North Sea in winter and it's never bothered me, but this one was all over the place. It must have been the movement and after a day I was ok. We were out in the Norwegian sector for three weeks. A good little job feeding twelve crew, and they did all the washing up for me in the galley after lunch and tea. A good crowd and the captain was a nice man. We came back in for dry dock for a week in Aberdeen and I put in a small store order but the office would not give me all that I asked for. Cut backs, apparently! The lads told me that when it was run and managed by the Norwegians you got more or less what you wanted, and as soon as a British management took over, it went downhill. I'm not surprised at all – it's like it's going back to the old days. After my four weeks, I got a flight home. That was October 2010.

I got another call a few weeks later to go and join the *Longstone* another ro-ro belonging to *Bibby's*. It was running between Finland, Sweden and Denmark. I went to Helsinki to join it. I was only on it about twelve days until the other cook came back. I flew home from Finland after that. Alan Banks was bosun on there and Dougie Hocking (from London originally) was AB. I had sailed with them on *Maersk* tankers 20 years ago. Alan is from Liverpool, and it was a nice little trip.

When I came off that I got another job on the Hurst Point a few weeks later. I think I flew out to Montreal to join it. Sean Finn from Middlesbrough was the bosun, and Chris the electrician was from Newcastle. Sean was a good laugh. We met up in Heathrow Airport and then flew out to Montreal. We stayed overnight in a hotel and then down to the ship next day. We went to the States again, then home. As I say, you hardly get any time in port these days and a lot of changes were going on – a big difference to what it was in the old days. You have just got to try and adapt to the changes – some good, some not.

Usually after a trip I like to go out to the Far East for a break. Mostly I go to Malaysia, as I said before, and to the Philippines. I love the people and the weather – can't beat it. I also have a lot of friends there. I stay at the Mariners' Centre in Penang which is central for me. I use it as a base and as I said, the people know me well there so when I am going out there, I phone them and let them know, so they come and pick me up at the airport. I always look forward to arriving there – it's a great feeling but it's a bit sad coming home, but there you go. I think it's more the bad weather we get at home, whereas out east it's always lovely. I always seem to be happy when the weather is nice – you can't have it both ways.

I got a job on a small survey boat, like a catamaran. There was only a crew of six on there but it can carry up to 16 with surveyors on board. It was a good little number – I was on it for about two months, just going out to Liverpool Bay and the wind farms. We then went around to Cherbourg and to Germany where I came off. Shortly after that I got a job on another survey boat, the *Cefas Endeavour*, a fishing trawler with a lot of scientists checking the fish quantities and different things about the fish they caught. I was on there a few weeks then came home.

I got a job on the *Hurst Point* a few weeks later. I had to take a flight to Muscat to join it. Angus McPherson was the captain so I knew him from before – a good captain who knew his job well. I think Sean Finn was the bosun, and I know I relieved Andy Cowely who got the sack over something. Anyway, I went out from Manchester Airport to Muscat, stayed in a hotel overnight and then down to the ship. The next day we sailed through the Suez Canal calling at Limassol and Taranto in Italy – a very nice place. Joe Nicholas was the second cook with me. We then went to Gibraltar and then to Marchwood. We had Christmas in Marchwood, which I didn't mind. I think I've had a few Christmases in Marchwood. I don't mind that – away from the hustle and bustle of ashore, nice peaceful time in port or at sea – whatever, I don't mind.

After Christmas we sailed down to the Falkland Islands calling at Ascension Island on the way. It's usually a round trip of about seven weeks so I got back to the UK in February 2012. I had my 65th birthday on 25th January 2012. I had just completed 50 years unbroken sea service from 1962 to 2012. I was hoping to get a few more trips in but I had a few medical problems that were coming back on me. On my way out to Malaysia for a holiday I had a strange feeling in my left eye. It was like a flying saucer going around so I went to a doctor in Malaysia. He said there was nothing much wrong so when I went to the Philippines to see my friend Gina (whom I have known for 16 years). We went to an eye specialist who said it was my lens which had been dislocated. Well, I have not seen out of my left eye since I was a boy – I've just had blurred vision but I got by. So when I got back to England I had to have a three-hour operation to remove the lens – a needle in my eye, local anaesthetic and three hours on my back. So I was off with that, and then I had to go and have a bladder operation that year in November. After that I got diagnosed with prostate cancer the second time, so I was up and down to hospitals and I could not go back to sea. In 2013 I had radiotherapy, and was very sick with after-effects. I have still not been able to get back to sea with all the hospital appointments I have. As they say, your health comes first – that is the lottery ticket, believe you me.

I am really struggling to come to terms with being ashore and not being able to go back to sea. And I was getting bouts of depression over it. I've always been doing something and going away to sea was my life. The only thing I wish is that I had met the right girl and had a family, but that was not to be. Maybe I do have someone I fathered somewhere in the world, I would not know! All in all I've had a great life, met some great people I sailed with, and some lovely girls. I suppose I could have settled down, but it wasn't to be, and when people say would you do it again, there is no question in my mind that I would.

Last year I was at my friend's daughter's wedding. Al Brown was a friend I went to sea with, and had a nice time, and Emma is his daughter. Then this year I was at Kitty Rice's youngest son Robert's daughter's wedding at the same place. That was also good – I met up with Tony Rice and Marty Rice (but not Michael) and funny enough I met the bridesmaid who was Robert's wife's cousin when they got married in August 1978 – a girl I dated, Kathy. I was Robert's best man then. She was lovely and glamorous then and still the same 35 years on – very bubbly and a happy go lucky girl. Looking back I say to myself, now what happened there? I did like Kathy a lot then, but we went our different ways and it was great to have a chat together, and lovely to see her after all these years.

I was at my brother's house the other day to see his wife Gill and daughter Lucy, who has two lovely children with Scott her husband, a boy and a girl. I also see my sister Ruth and her daughter Lindsay. She has a young son, Joel. Ruth's son is a teacher in China. I haven't seen my other sister Kathleen for a while but I am in touch. She has a son and a daughter who are married, young Keith and Louise. Kath's husband Keith is a lorry driver and Ruth's husband Dave is retired, a bit like myself now. I also have a lot of cousins in Liverpool. I see Colette and Maria, Paul and their families and the Sullivans and O'Donohues, so we do see each other often. My brother's son James went to Oxford and is a consultant histo-pathologist. He has done very well.

It was about 1971 when I first met Tony Rice, a seaman, in town in a pub called the Pen and Whig. Anyway he took me home to his house and that's how I met his mum and dad, Kitty and Marty Rice, and his brothers. I was friends with the family for 30-odd years. They used to call me the fifth son. Kitty was a great woman, kind and generous. She even gave me a key to her house to stay if I had been out on the town, rather than having to go home to Halewood. I was always down at the house when I was home from sea. We would all go out for a drink. Marty was in the engine room on the ship. He was a funny man. Unfortunately they have both passed away – wonderful people whose memories I cherished. They lived in Windsor Street in the south end of Liverpool and we always went up to Park Road to drink – some great pubs up there, and great people. I ended up sailing with Tony Rice and our other mate Sid Maloney on the *Ceramic* in 1972, a *Shaw Saville* ship out to Kiwi and Australia. Sid passed away years ago but I see his wife who works in *Tesco* in Aigburth Rd. Her name is Joyce, a lovely woman.

There used to be a place at the bottom of Park Lane called the Seamen's Dispensary. Now that's a posh name, and I'll leave it to the reader to work out what it was for. I remember Kitty Rice telling me that she used to have a pub in Park Lane called the Liver and a lot of seamen drank there who knew Kitty. During the 1960 strike she looked after them and they never forgot her. There was a place around the corner where the seamen signed off and on the ships called Cornhill. Anyway, getting back to the story, someone had broken into the Dispensary and the seamen's personal files were all over the place. I don't know if it's true, but a lot of the girls were looking at the names of the listed visitors to the Dispensary. I heard that some of the fellas never came around to the Liver pub 'til it had all calmed down. The nickname for the dispensary was 'Dr Ross's' as he was known to the seamen. I was in the Docker's Club years ago in Liverpool, the Casa, and one of the dockers got up on the stage to say to the audience that he had received some sad news. "Dr Ross has just passed away," he said, "so let's please have a minute's silence for him." After that I heard one wife say to another lady, "Who the hell's Dr Ross?" "Oh," she replied, "he was just a well known doctor among the seamen's fraternity." Then this fella shouted over, "It wasn't just the seamen he befriended either!" Everyone burst out laughing.

I am still in touch with Tony Lloyd from Salford. He calls me when he comes home, or I go to visit him in Salford. Chris Cullen, another good friend of mine, calls me regularly to see how I am. I went on a few marches for the seamen with him. I see lads I have known for years. Eddie Devlin and his wife Eileen, who are good people; Fred Bradley, Denny Vaz, George Murray, Hugh and Marie Carragher; Marty Hand, a good friend with his wife Denise, great people; Mark Wong and Charlotte, who have been good to me; also Alby and June Brown; Adam and Emma, my god-daughter, who I go and see regularly – Emma has two young boys, now married to Steve; Derek Creed I've known a long time and Billy Ando, and also Darren Ireland and his wife Andrea; Bobby Dicko, Joe Dobbs, George and Dave Leonard, Tony Harrison, Peter Hall, Billy Murray and his wife Liz – I sailed with Tony Harrison on the *Ellerman* ship *Arcadian* and Billy Anderson in *Blue Star Line*.

I also have cousins on my father's side of the family who live down south – Dad's sisters Doreen and Kath and cousins in the USA who I visited a few years ago. Also, one of my neighbours from where I used to live – Jo was her name. She always used to ring me when I was ill, a lovely girl who has been through a lot herself but she just gets on in life. Eddie Owen and his wife, Margaret, and family have been very good to me, and especially Eddie's grandson, Michael Gould. I go back a long time with Eddie in the *Blue Star Line* and he has brought his family up well. You can see that has rubbed off on his grandson Michael. Great people. I have some great memories of going up to see Eddie in the Holy Name Social Club in Fazakerly. There were some great characters I met there in the 1980s when I used to come home from sea.

I have also lost a few mates these last few years. John Peeney and Joe Boyle, both seamen and great characters, and recently Jimmy Rourke, a seaman also. We gave him a good send off. In the early chapter of my book I mentioned Christy O'Donohue and my father's sister Margret Tipton, who since then both have passed away.

I've been back to hospital and I am clear again, so still have to go back every month for checks, but I feel fine. In fact I have been doing a bit of relief work up in the North Sea on supply boats and that has helped me a lot getting over my illness and I was back to my old self eating well and keeping fit.

In 2013 my cancer returned after my PSA levels were high, so it was decided that I was to have a six week course of radiotherapy. Before all that I had an operation on my bladder. The doctors were a bit reluctant to go ahead with the radiotherapy, as it might have damaged the work that they had done on the bladder as it was around that area that I was to have the radiotherapy. Anyway, I had the bladder operation in London. Before that I had to have the lens removed out of my left eye.

I started the course of radiotherapy. I used to travel to Aintree Hospital on the bus and train every day for six weeks (not weekends). Everything was fine. When I finished the day of radiotherapy I would go and meet friends for a coffee. Eventually I finished the treatment. At that time I was under four different hospitals – London Middlesex, McMillan Cancer Clinic London, Liverpool Linda McCartney Clinic and Aintree Hospital. It wasn't until weeks after I started to lose my appetite – did not want to read papers or watch TV, or talk to anyone. I was feeling really down – not like me. I went to my doctor and he said I had depression, so he put me on a course of anti-depressants. I had lost a bit of weight as well. For those who don't know what depression is about, it is a bad thing. Mine was brought on by the effects of the radiotherapy, and also I was trying to come to terms with finishing with the sea as I have never done anything else. All my life I have been a seafarer – for 50 years. The only break was when I was getting my treatments, and it is really hard to settle and readjust to shore life.

After about six weeks I started to get back to my old self, and the first thing I did was to get back on the ships again so I got a job on a standby boat up in the North Sea. Four weeks on, and four weeks off. Ideal for me! The doctor did not want me to go back deep sea much as I would have liked. Anyway, I was content with this job. You know what, after a day on the ship, my spirits lifted. I was like a new man. This is where I belong, the noise of the engines, the galley and the hustle and bustle of the crew going about their work. It is a strange thing to say I was not worried about my illnesses. I'm not the kind to worry, but I was worried that I could not get back to work on the ships.

The ship was old, the cabin very small, it wasn't the *Hilton*. It had a TV and a shower and I was as happy as a pig in shit, as they say – would not have swapped it for the world. That was my therapy for getting well. I've put on weight and I only have to go for check-ups once a year thanks to our wonderful NHS staff, from cleaners to nurses and doctors – we are so lucky to have it.

I go on my holidays to Malaysia every year, which does me good. After my treatment I met a lady from Saudi Arabia who was to become a good friend. Her name is Jouharha. It was in a coffee bar in Bold Street run by Sam – a great place and coffee with wonderful staff. Anyway we got talking and she told me she was studying at the university in Liverpool, all paid for by the Saudi Government. She is married and has three boys – Thamer who is twelve, Ayad who is eight and Wesam who is six. The kids are very polite and they always call me 'Mr Eddie' when they see me. They all speak with a Liverpool accent now, and they love Liverpool. She is very open about things and we have some interesting conversations about different subjects and the world in general. She dresses very stylishly and is a lovely person. Of course, whether she is in Liverpool or Saudi Arabia, she puts on the Hijab. She loves being in Liverpool and feels it as her second home – she always looks forward to coming back to Liverpool when she goes to visit her family in Saudi Arabia.

We share so many things and interests in common, so we became close friends. She is an open-minded and respectful of other cultures. She takes the kids to school, then goes to university, then picks them up. She goes for coffee before that. She knows all the girls who work there and has a very good sense of humour.

One particular day near Christmas she asked me to meet her and her kids after she picked them up from school, and on the way back one of them was singing Christmas carols and they had drawings they showed me of the Christmas festivities they had done. Their mother was smiling as I looked at her as the kid carried on singing. He is only eight years old. Even though Christmas is not a part of their culture, they like going down to town to enjoy the atmosphere and watch the lights and decorations. The mother and Ayad are very happy when it snows, so they are the first out of their house when it snows. And lastly, she has been more than helpful in getting my autobiography together.

You get to met people from all walks of life in the Bold St coffee bar – a lot of musicians and actors, actresses and writers.

Sometimes you will see the odd footballer there. Julianna is a lady from Brazil I know who goes there. She lives in Liverpool and organises events like Brazilian dancing that she participates in and other events. A lovely person and always smiling. John Montgomery is another friend of mine. He is an illustrator and very talented. He went to art school in Liverpool. I met his mother and sister. His mother grew up in Liverpool with my mother's sister and knew the family very well.

I was recently at a seamen's reunion in North Wales with the lads who I sailed within the *Blue Star Line*. We had a great time there meeting lads I sailed with years ago: Lee Petts, Neil McBride, Mick Brown, Jimmy Derbyshire, Vince Cowie, Chris Mulaney – so many there. Steve Tyley organised it and he did a great job bringing us altogether with a lovely dinner. An old friend of mine came over from New Zealand. Her name is Moana and she stayed with me. She really enjoyed herself – I showed her around Liverpool and the Wirral before she went back to New Zealand.

I do see some of the lads I sailed with in the past. I went up to see John Doyle and his wife Mary. They live in Halewood. I sailed with John way back in the late 1970s. I took him a painting of the *Hobart Star*, as he was on there. John was on deck – I think it was down in Lyttleton on the *Ulster Star*. I had left my transformer on there – it's a machine for alternating the electrical current, and you needed one of them on the old ships for cassette players – they were like gold dust. Anyway, they sent it down to me in Lyttleton. You don't need them on the ships today. When we used to join ships in the USA we would take all our music with us – speakers, cassettes and players. The crew bar was like the She club in Liverpool. When we were on the New Zealand coast everyone loved the *Hobart Star*. It was very popular with everyone, the party ship. John's mates were Arthur ward, Tommy Fullerton, Kenny Carroll and John Lewy – the 'Wild Bunch' – they played hard and worked hard. Just recently I bumped into another seafarer, Gorge Neath, who has been ill but it was good to see him up and about. I sailed with Gorge on the container ship *ACT One* in 1978.

I am eventually going to have to finish working and going to sea. Gradually I hope I will get used to it. A lot of people often asked me why I never ever married. Well, I guess I enjoyed the life of wandering from one place to another on the oceans and suppose never met the right one. I used to say to myself, in comparison to a bee, why land in the centre of the honey pot and get stuck there when you can just fly away and land on the side of many others and still taste the honey – anytime, anywhere, without getting stuck! That's, in seaman's terms I would say, 'to the reader's conclusion'.

I was up to see an old ship mate in the nursing home, Jimmy Foo, who is a lovely man. He was cook in *Lamport and Holt Lines* for years. I took Eddie Owens, a friend of ours, up to see him. He seemed a bit confused – he is 92 years of age but as we started talking about the past and the men we sailed with, Jimmy came alive listening. It really does him good when someone visits him – he said to Eddie, "You never change, you still look the same." Eddie first met Jimmy in 1957, Eddie is 82 now. Anyway, it was good to see him and I will continue to visit him. We also visit another old shipmate, George Murray.

I did a Christmas trip on one of the standby boats I was on in 2014. We had just come from Norway to go on location in the North Sea. The weather was bad, the ship rocking all over the place, and trying to cook was a nightmare. If it gets too bad, you just put on something easy as it can be very dangerous in the galley. Christmas was approaching and the captain told me the weather would be OK, so I would be able to put a Christmas dinner in, which I did, and it went down very well with everyone full and happy. The next trip I did on the same ship. When I went back, I happened to mention to the captain that the company never paid me the Christmas bonus. As everyone else got it, he was surprised that I never got it. Anyway, the next day they had a safety meeting on the bridge where everyone attended. After the meeting was over, Neil the boatswain (a really nice fella from Hull would do anything for you and always helped me on odd jobs I needed doing) mentioned to the captain that the crew was not happy that I had not been included in getting the Christmas bonus. As Neil stated,

"Eddie the cook is part of the crew and in any emergency, man overboard, rig education, Eddie is part of the team that will help survivors and we feel that he should have been paid his bonus." I said to them, "Thank you for your concern but I'm not bothered about it to that extent." But they asked the captain to send an email asking why the cook never got a Christmas bonus. A few days later, the captain came down to the mess room with the reply to the email from a person stating that he was surprised that it was brought up after the safety meeting, and said that because I got the job off the agency I was not entitled to the Christmas bonus. Obviously he had no idea how to liaise with crew members on a ship. I was doing the same job as my back-to-back cook and I was on far less salary – as the agency takes a big cut, that's the way it is now. The company always flies the crews up to Aberdeen and the same going home, but then someone in the office decided that only the officers could get a taxi from the airport to the vessel. The crew would have to get the bus. Well it's time to get out – it has gone right back in time to class distinction, even when there are only twelve crew members on the ship. We face the everyday dangers of the sea and the elements of the weather. The lads that take the fast craft rescue boat out in the heavy seas in an emergency in no time are prepared. Out in the boats on exercises heading out to the rig on a man overboard, they bring him back in no time safely for the rest of the crew to give first-aid. They put their lives at risk to help others and the company come out with the class distinction over the taxis and buses – disgraceful. Everyone has a part to play on the ship and a seaman will always look out for his shipmate.

You know, they go on about health and safety but when it comes to spending money on some issues, the safety goes out the window. The company I was with was *Norwegian* and they are renowned for having modern ships – even their old tonnage was of a high standard. Regarding accommodation and conditions, I remember the crew on one ship saying to me, "You know what, Eddie, when the *Norwegian* office was crewing the ships, the standard was high and plenty of stores, food and good wages, and as soon as the British take over management it's gone downhill with all the cuts."

"Well," I said, "that's nothing new." That's why I always say you should be in the union, to make sure you get good conditions and pay. It's sad really to see the way the industry has gone.

Early in 2015 I went out to Penang, Malaysia. I had just done a few trips up the North Sea on a standby boat. It was winter time and the weather was really bad up there, so going out to Penang for a few months would be a nice break. I also went over to Brisbane, Australia, to visit a lady friend of mine and my sister Ruth who grew up with us kids in the prefabs in Belle Vale. Her name is Lal and her parents emigrated to Australia in 1957. They lived next door to us. It was really nice to meet up after 50-odd years. 1957 was the last time I had seen her. I had a nice time, met her husband and her sister Grace (who I did not remember as she was older). She and her husband are in their eighties now. They remembered me and Ruth when we were very young, and of course my parents. When they left for Australia, my mother was very upset as Lal's mother and father were close friends. I tried to find them in the 1970s when I was on a ship in Brisbane but had no luck until Facebook two years ago. How things work out! I stayed in Brisbane for eight days and enjoyed it. There have been a lot of changes since I was last there. I went back to Malaysia to finish off my holiday, then came home.

A few months later another friend got in touch with me who was my mate growing up in the prefabs and I went to school with. His name was Peter Cowperthwait. When we left school, I went to sea and he went into the army, 'The Greenjackets' regiment. I had not seen him since the sixties. We met up and my sister came over to Liverpool as she knew him and we had lunch and a chat about our schooldays. It was great to see him and his wife Anne.

I've just got 53 years in now at sea and when I look back I've had the best years of my life with some great people. So now I'm going in the dry dock for the last time and to call it a day as the ocean nomad.

Eddie Bolton
2015

S/S "ROLAND" APPROXIMATE VOYAGE ITINERARY. LIST No.2 II 14/12/69

PORT.	ARRIVE		SAIL		LAST POSTING DATE.	
BUENOS AIRES.	NOV	29	DEC	16	- -	
PARANAGUA	DEC	19	DEC	21	- -	
SANTOS	DEC	22	DEC	24	- -	
RECIFE	DEC	28	DEC	31	DEC	20
CAPETOWN	JAN	10	JAN	10	CALL UNCERTAIN.	
EAST LONDON	JAN	12	JAN	12	- -	
DURBAN	JAN	13	JAN	14	JAN	6
SINGAPORE	JAN	26	JAN	29	JAN	21
HONG KONG	FEB	3	FEB	4	JAN	27
KEELUNG	FEB	6	FEB	6	- -	
1ST JAPANESE PORT	FEB	8	- - - - - - - - - - - - - - -			

THIS LIST IS AN ESTIMATION AND IS SUBJECT TO CHANGE. MORE
DETAILS WILL BE PASSED ON AS INFORMATION IS RECEIVED.

S/S "ROLAND" APPROXIMATE ITINERARY SUBJECT TO ALTERATION.

POSTING DATES AND ADDRESSES DATE 3RD FEBRUARY,1970 LIST No.4.

PORT	ARRIVE		SAIL		LAST POSTING DATE	
HONG KONG	FEB	7	FEB	9	- -	
KOBE / OSAKA	FEB	13	FEB	15	- -	
NAGOYA	FEB	16	FEB	16	- -	
YOKOHAMA	FEB	17	FEB	19	- -	
YAWATA / MOJI	FEB	21	FEB	22	- -	
SINGAPORE	MAR	2	MAR	3	FEB	23
PENANG	MAR	4	MAR	5	- -	
L/MARQUES	MAR	23	MAR	24	MAR	15
DURBAN	MAR	26	MAR	28	MAR	18
RECIFE	CALL POSSIBLE.					
RIO DE JANEIRO	APR	5	APR	8	MAR	26
SANTOS	APR	4	APR	13	APR	25
BUENOS AIRES	APR	15	NOT KNOWN.		APR	15

EXPECT TO LOAD RIVER PLATE AND BRASIL FOR U.K. — WHERE DUE
SECOND HALF MAY.

SINGAPORE	AUSTASIA LINE LTD., P.O. BOX 1946, SINGAPORE, 1, SINGAPORE.
PENANG	ANGLO FRENCH TRADING CO.LTD., PENANG, MALAYA.
L/MARQUES	J.M.BARNETT & CO. LTD., P.O. BOX 1614, LOURENCO MARQUES, MOZAMBIQUE.
DURBAN	GUNDELFINGER & SON, P.O. BOX 1477, DURBAN, SOUTH AFRICA.
RIO.D.J.	CIA. EXPRESSO MERCANTIL, CAIXA POSTAL 969 - Ze - CO, RIO DE JANEIRO, BRASIL.
SANTOS	CIA EXPRESSO MERCANTIL, CAIXA POSTAL 445, SANTOS SAO PAULO, BRASIL.
Bs. As.	BLUE STAR LINE DE LA ARGENTINA, CASILLA DE CORREO 997, BUENOS AIRES, ARGENTINA.

Crusader Line
New Zealand Direct Service

OVERSEAS SHIPPING COMPANY, GENERAL AGENTS
ONE CALIFORNIA STREET, SAN FRANCISCO, CALIFORNIA 94111
CABLE ADDRESS "OVERSEAS" TELETYPE: 910-372-6017 TELEPHONE (415) 956-2114
Inbound —Pier 27 Outbound—Pier 48 B 1/10/

	Fremantel Star V. 48	Hobart Star V. 52	Timaru Star V. 36	Fremantle Star V. 50	Hobart Star V. 54
Wellington		Sailed	Sailed	Jan 31	Mar 14
Lyttleton	Sailed	Sailed	Sailed	Jan 23	Mar 6
Dunedin	Sailed			Jan 25	
New Plymouth	Sailed	Sailed	Jan 11	Feb 4	Mar 18
Napier			Sailed	Feb 7	Mar 21
Auckland	Sailed	Sailed	Sailed	Feb 14	Mar 28
Levuka		Sailed		Feb 18	Apr 1
Honolulu	Sailed	Sailed	Feb 3	Feb 25	Apr 8
Los Angeles	Sailed	Jan 15	Feb 18	Mar 4	Apr 15
San Francisco	Sailed	Jan 17	Feb 22	Mar 7	Apr 18
Tacoma	Sailed	Jan 20-21	Feb 16-17	Mar 10-12	Apr 21-22
	Fremantle V49	Hobart V.53	Timaru V.37	Fremantl V.51	Hobart V.55
Vancouver, B.C.	Sailed	Jan 23-24	Feb 10-15	Mar 13-14	Apr 24-25
San Francisco	Sailed	Jan 30	Feb 23	Mar 21	May 2
Los Angeles	Sailed	Jan 28	Feb 19	Mar 18	Apr 29
Fiji (Suva)	Sailed	Feb 13	Mar 8	Apr 3	May 15
Auckland	Jan 10	Feb 17	Mar 13	Apr 7	May 19
Wellington	Jan 27	Mar 10	Apr 10	Apr 28	Jun 9
Lyttleton	Jan 20	Mar 3	Apr 3	Apr 21	Jun 2
Dunedin	Jan 24				Jun 6
Bluff		Mar 7			
New Plymouth	Feb 1	Mar 15	Apr 16	May 3	Jun 14
Napier	Feb 6	Mar 20	Apr 20	May 8	Jun 19

m.v.Mairangi Bay.　　　　　　　Voyage 72.

Around the World in 80 Days.

Passage Tilbury to Hamburg.	1 day	12 mins.	Dist. 418 mls.
Alongside Hamburg.	1 day	8 hours 42 mins.	
Passage Hamburg to Rotterdam.		21 hours	Dist. 332 mls.
Alongside Rotterdam.	1 day	5 hours 24 mins.	
Passage Rotterdam to Fremantle.	25 days	14 hours 54 mins.	Dist. 10999 mls.
Alongside Fremantle.	1 day	10 hours 6 mins.	
Passage Fremantle to Adelaide.	2 days	19 hours 48 mins.	Dist. 1382 mls.
Alongside Adelaide.	1 day	11 hours 48 mins.	
Passage Adelaide to Melbourne.		21 hours 6 mins.	Dist. 514 mls.
Alongside Melbourne.		21 hours 48 mins.	
Passage Melbourne to Burnie.		13 hours 54 mins.	Dist. 225 mls.
Alongside Burnie.		16 hours 42 mins.	
Passage Burnie to Sydney.	1 day	2 hours 18 mins.	Dist. 514 mls.
Alongside Sydney.	2 days	2 hours 6 mins.	
Passage Sydney to Auckland.	2 days	16 hours	Dist. 1282 mls.
Alongside Auckland.		16 hours	
Passage Auckland to Wellington.	1 day	5 hours 48 mins.	Dist. 557 mls.
Alongside Wellington.	1 day	10 hours 36 mins.	
Passage Wellington to Lyttelton.		13 hours 6 mins.	Dist. 173 mls.
Alongside Lyttelton.	1 day	4 hours 6 mins.	
Passage Lyttelton to Port Chalmers.		11 hours 54 mins.	Dist. 197 mls.
Alongside Port Chalmers.	2 days	12 hours	
Passage Port Chalmers to Lisbon.	23 days	16 hours 42 mins.	Dist. 11217 mls
Alongside Lisbon.		7 hours 12 mins.	
Passage Lisbon to Zeebrugge.	2 days	22 hours 54 mins.	Dist. 1071 mls.
Alongside Zeebrugge.		11 hours 12 mins.	
Passage Zeebrugge to Tilbury.		11 hours 6 mins.	Dist. 136 mls.

The vessel crossed the Equator Southbound in longitude 9'16.2'W on 7/4/95 @ 0600 hours.
Crossed the Equator Northbound in longitude 28'40'W on 4/6/95 @ 2320 hours.

Homeward bound voyage crossed outward bound voyage in position Twenty Eight Degrees North , Sixteen Degrees West , between the Islands of Gran Canaria and Tenerife , on Thursday 8th June @ 1900 hours.

Total Voyage distance　; 29017 nautical miles.
Total Voyage time　　　; 80 days, 16 hours, 24 minutes.

LAMPORT & HOLT LINE

ON BOARD _S/S "ROLAND"_

18TH NOVEMBER, 19___.

ARRIVING MONTEVIDEO 26/11/69.

NOTICE TO ALL CREW MEMBERS.

THE FOLLOWING INFORMATION HAS BEEN RECEIVED BY ME TODAY FROM LAMPORT AND HOLT LINE (LIVERPOOL) :-

AFTER DISCHARGE OF CARGO IN BUENOS AIRES THIS VESSEL IS GOING ON CHARTER. WE WILL BE LOADING A CARGO IN BRASIL FOR JAPAN VIA CAPETOWN, SINGAPORE AND HONG KONG. AFTER DISCHARGE IN JAPAN A RETURN CARGO WILL BE LOADED TO SOUTH AMERICA, WHERE THE CHARTER WILL END. VESSEL WILL THEN LOAD FOR HOME.

THIS IS EXPECTED TO MAKE THE VOYAGE ABOUT 3½ MONTHS LONGER. I HAVE NO DETAILS YET BUT I SHOULD THINK VESSEL SHOULD BE HOME END OF APRIL / BEGINNING OF MAY.

AS SOON AS DETAILS ARE RECEIVED BY ME I WILL POST UP A LIST OF ADDRESSES AND POSTING DATES TO BE USED ON THE CHARTERED VOYAGE.

ANYONE WISHING TO ADJUST ALLOTMENTS OR SEND EXTRA MONEY HOME BECAUSE OF THESE CHANGES CAN DO SO BY SEEING ME AT A SUITABLE TIME.

W.A. SPARKS, MASTER.

M.V. Peninsular Bay   Christmas 1993

Christmas Dinner

Chilled Fruit Juice
Chilled Melon Boats
Consomme Royal   Cream of Tomato Soup
Prawn Cocktail Marie Louise Sauce

xxxxxxxxxxxxxxxxx

Grilled Salmon Darne Hollandaise Sauce
Ham Mushroom Vol Au Vents
Baked Ginger and Honey Glazed Ham
Roast Norfolk Turkey
Cranberry Sauce and Stuffing
Grilled Medallion Boeuf, Chasseur

xxxxxxxxxxxxxxxxx

Roast Potatoes, Duchess Potatoes
Sliced Carrots Brussels Sprouts

xxxxxxxxxxxxxxxxx

Steamed Plum Pudding Brandy Sauce
Sherry Fruit Trifle
Black Forest Gateaux Ice Cream

xxxxxxxxxxxxxxxxx

Cheese Board, Biscuits, Bread Rolls
Mince Pies, Assorted Nuts, Fresh Fruit
Yule Logs   Christmas Cake

xxxxxxxxxxxxxxxxx

Bon Appetite   Eddie, Cook/Stwd

M.V. AVELONA STAR

EMERGENCY STATIONS

BRIDGE PARTY

MASTER	J. IGOE
2ND OFF	J. WILLIS-RICHARDS
RADIO OFF	I. ACLAND-MARTIN
WHEELMAN	J. ROURKE

EMERGENCY DECK PARTY		EMERGENCY ENGINEROOM PARTY	
CHIEF OFFICER	C. BUFTON	2ND. ENG.	J. PARTRIDGE
3RD OFFICER	R. SAVAGE	5TH. ENG.	R. SWIFT
C.P.O. DECK	J. MACINNES	P.O.M.M.	G. OWENS
S.M.1.A.	D. SINCLAIR	M.M.1.A.	P. NAGBERI
S.M.1.A.	T. BELLIS	M.M.1.A.	P. HAYS
S.M.1.B.	R. MEELIND		

STRETCHER PARTY		IN ENGINEROOM	
2ND STEWARD	M. SAVAGE	CHIEF ENG.	A. SOWARD
ASS. STEWARD	F. RAY	3RD. ENG	D. WAINWRIGHT
ASS. STEWARD	I. JONES	ELECTRICIAN	J. DOWD
ASS. STEWARD	A. SCOTT		
ASS. STEWARD	P. LORIMER		

TO PREPARE BOATS		TO COLLECT PROVISIONS FROM BRIDGE AND ASSIST AS DIRECTED	
CARPENTER	W. NEIL		
4TH. ENG.	D. ASHTON	2ND COOK	D. GRIFFITHS
S.M.1.A.	S. OWEN	2ND COOK	T. FLAHERTY
S.M.1.D.	G. BARKER		
S.M.2.	P. MOONEY		

I/C HOSPITAL & AFTER DECK LIASON		I/C GALLEY	
PURSER	B. BOWLER	CHIEF COOK	E. BOLTON

M.O.D. PERSONNEL

I/C D. MOREMENT S. T.O.(N)

ALL PERSONNEL TO ACT AS REQUIRED / DIRECTED

EMERGENCY STATIONS SIGNAL

CONTINOUS RINGING OF ALARM BELLS, CONTINOUS SOUNDING OF SHIPS WHISTLE, SPOKEN WORDS OVER P.A. SYSTEM TO HOLDS " HANDS TO MUSTER STATIONS "
ACTION
ON HEARING EMERGENCY SIGNAL ALL PERSONNEL TO MUSTER ON THE AFTERDECK FOR HEAD COUNT FROM DEPARTMENTAL HEADS. ON COMPLETION OF HEAD COUNT ALL PERSONNEL TO PROCEED TO THIER EMERGENCY STATION.

HARD HATS, SUITABLE CLOTHING I.E. LONG SLEEVED SHIRTS, LONG TROUSERS & STOUT BOOTS OR SHOES SHOULD BE WARN

LIFEJACKETS TO BE CARRIED TO MUSTER STATIONS

TELEPHONE 01-488 4567
01-481 8971

TELEGRAMS BLUESTARLI, LONDON, TELEX
TELEX N° LONDON 888298

BLUE STAR LINE
LTD.

IN REPLYING PLEASE
QUOTE REFERENCE

ALBION HOUSE,
LEADENHALL STREET,
LONDON, EC3A 1AR.

8th July, 1974.

Dear Sir,

JOINING INSTRUCTIONS

M.V. "HOBART STAR" AT LOS ANGELES

You will be proceeding from Gatwick Airport by a scheduled flight of British Caledonian Airlines to Los Angeles, with the following flight schedule:-

FLIGHT BR 221

Check in at Gatwick Airport:	10.30 hours, THURSDAY, 11th July
Departs Gatwick Airport:	11.30 hours, THURSDAY, 11th July
Arrives Los Angeles Airport:	15.00 hours, THURSDAY, 11th July

(All times are local time)

Coach transport will be provided to Gatwick Airport, departing from Blue Star Line 'Z' Berth, Royal Victoria Dock Office at 08.00 hours THURSDAY, 11th July - PROMPT.

You may also proceed direct to Gatwick Airport where you should arrive not later than 10.30 hours.

On arrival at Los Angeles, overnight accommodation will be provided and you should therefore take with you on the flight, an overnight bag.

DOCUMENTS REQUIRED:-   (these documents should be carried with you and NOT LOCKED IN YOUR CASE)

1.   British Seaman's Identity Card and / or valid British Passport (with a valid USA Visa inside).

2.   New-style British Seaman's Discharge Book.

3.   Valid International Certificate of Vaccination against Smallpox.

Your acknowledgement of receipt of these instructions to your Superintendent would be appreciated, advising at the same time, whether you will be joining the coach at the Dock Office or proceeding direct to London Airport.

Yours faithfully,
BLUE STAR LINE LIMITED

CREW MANAGER
Fleet Personnel Department.

Collected by D. MacKinnon   1974.

M/V"HOBART STAR"

ART. No.		NAME.	RANK.	DI.A.No.	D.O.B.	NATIONALITY.
I.		D.J. ECKWORTH.	MASTER.	R923484.	16- 5-37.	"BRITISH"
58.		D. CRADDOCK.	CH.OFF.	R717598.	I- 3-42.	"BRITISH"
3.		D. KELLIHER.	2. OFF.	R880597.	4- 7-51.	"IRISH"
4.		D. WOOD.	3.OFF.	UKOI4808.	6- 4-51.	"BRITISH"
5.		P. JARVIS.	CADET.	UK009873.	I- 2-55.	"BRITISH"
59.		J. KAY.	CADET.	UK009203.	15- I-56.	"BRITISH"
7.		T. LEE.	R.OFF.	R867070.	16- /-47.	"IRISH"
8.		G. HENDERSON.	CH.ENG.	RI75881.	4-12-13.	"BRITISH"
9.		F. FRECH.	2.ENG.	R867905.	22- 2-49.	"AUSTRALIAN"
4.		R. DELLOW.	3.ENG.	R847766.	13- 9-45.	"BRITISH"
II.		N. ANDERSON.	4.ENG.	H450481.	30-11-52.	"AUSTRALIAN"
I2.		J. FROST.	5.ENG.	H667697.	3- 9-50.	"AUSTRALIAN"
60.		R. ROWLANDS.	J.ENG.	H879433.	7- 6-52.	"AUSTRALIAN"
I4.		P. SCOTT.	C.R.ENG.	R750344.	24- 6-15.	"BRITISH"
I5.		J. LANG.	CH.ELEC.	R64670I.	27- 8-38.	"BRITISH"
I6.		T. MARSHALL.	2.ELEC.	UK028959.	22- 4-54.	"BRITISH"
I7.		J. SPANSWICK.	E.CADET.	UKOI2079.	I- 5-55.	"BRITISH"
I8.		P. JACKSON.	E.CADET.	UK032072.	I4- 4-57.	"BRITISH"
56.		D. JOHNSTON.	T. OFF.	UK029346.	II-II-52.	"BRITISH"
I9.	20	J.T. HEFFERNAN.	P.C.O.	R663778.	I3- 4-38.	"IRISH"
2I.	5	C. DONNELLY.	CARP.	R547364.	22-IO-22.	"BRITISH"
22.	10	D. MacKINNON.	BOSUN.	R773534.	22- 2-46.	"BRITISH"
23.	10	K. MAUNDER.	A.B.	R869809.	23- 4-52.	"BRITISH"
24.	10	G. HENDRICH.	A.B.	R900643.	25- 5-44.	"BRITISH"
25.	10	J. LEWIS.	A.B.	R727425.	29-I2-43.	"BRITISH"
26.	5	G. ANTHONY.	E.D.H.	R9I2006.	I8-I2-54.	"BRITISH"
27.	10	P. WARD.	E.D.H.	R753870.	5- 3-45.	"BRITISH"
28.	10	T. FULLERTON.	E.D.H.	R862526.	26-I2-52.	"BRITISH"
29.	10	C. ROBINSON.	A.B.	R785354.	6- 9-46.	"BRITISH"
30.	—	A. MacKINNON.	A.B.	R6I5555.	7- 5-38.	"BRITISH"
32.	10	K. CARROLL.	D.H.U.	UKO24186.	3- 9-59.	"BRITISH"
33.	5	C. DEAN.	D.BOY.	UK025689.	IO- 3-58.	"BRITISH"
34.	5	D. BULL.	MECH.	UKOI9306.	II-II-44.	"BRITISH"
35.	5	R. STEELE.	MECH.	UK022278.	8- 6-55.	"BRITISH"
36.	10	D. MacNEIL.	D.MAN.	R5I3744.	28-IO-3I.	"BRITISH"
38.	10	J. IRWIN.	D.GRS.	R593396.	I4-I2-27.	"BRITISH"
39.	5	F. KNOX.	D.GRS.	RI29343.	I5- 6-I6.	"BRITISH"
40.	5	W. KOZAK.	D.GRS.	R877695.	4-IO-44.	"BRITISH"
4I.	10	J. RYAN.	D.GRS.	R308833.	25- 4-26.	"BRITISH"
42.	—	K. PALUCHA.	D.GRS.	R364257.	I- I-I6.	"BRITISH"
53.	5	J. SCORGIE.	D.GRS.	R403459.	23-IO-22.	"IRISH"
43.	10	D. McGEE.	CLNR.	R77592I.	30- 7-49.	"BRITISH"
44.	10	E. BAKER.	2.STWD.	UKG08I58.	II-II-34.	"BRITISH"
45.	—	E. BOLTON.	CH.COOK.	R778537.	25- I-47.	"BRITISH"
46.	10	R. TAYLOR.	2.CK.B.	R29I365.	5-IO-27.	"BRITISH"
47.	10	S. WHITEHURST.	CKS.ASST.	UKOI3860.	5- 6-55.	"BRITISH"
48.	5	A. ELLIOTT.	A.STWD.	R870035.	I7- I-53.	"BRITISH"
49.	5	J. SALINAS.	A.STWD.	R863959.	II- 4-52.	"BRITISH"
50.	5	D. McCLENNAN.	A.STWD.	R860II0.	2- 9-52.	"BRITISH"
5I.	5	D. HENDERSON.	A.STWD.	UK02I8I3.	24- 5-45.	"BRITISH"
52.	10	G. DUMBELL.	M.MAN.	RI68976.	7- 3-16.	"BRITISH"
E.I.		J. ECKWORTH.	Mrs.	K737703A.		"BRITISH"
E.2.		D. HENDERSON.	Mrs.	I98244.		"BRITISH"
E.3.		A. WOOD.	Mrs.	H69I764.		"AUSTRALIAN"
E.4.		A. FRECH.	Mrs.	H8I0052.		"AUSTRALIAN"

$240.00 N.Z

22.00 N.Z — M.U.S.   £121 38   Crew

$262.00   122.62½   Pay Off

m.v. KOWLOON BAY — MAILING LIST

PORT	ARRIVES	DEPARTS	LAST MAILING DATE
ALGECIRAS	21-Aug-95	21-Aug-95	14-Aug-95
MALTA	24-Aug-95	24-Aug-95	17-Aug-95
SUEZ CANAL	26-Aug-95	27-Aug-95	16-Aug-95
JEDDAH	29-Aug-95	30-Aug-95	19-Aug-95
JEBEL ALI	04-Sep-95	05-Sep-95	25-Aug-95
NHAVA SHEVA	08-Sep-95	10-Sep-95	29-Aug-95
SUEZ CANAL	17-Sep-95	17-Sep-95	07-Sep-95
MALTA	19-Sep-95	20-Sep-95	09-Sep-95
ALGECIRAS	22-Sep-95	23-Sep-95	12-Sep-95
HALIFAX	30-Sep-95	30-Sep-95	20-Sep-95
NEW YORK	02-Oct-95	03-Oct-95	22-Sep-95
MIAMI	05-Oct-95	05-Oct-95	25-Sep-95
HOUSTON	07-Oct-95	08-Oct-95	27-Sep-95
CHARLESTON	11-Oct-95	11-Oct-95	01-Oct-95
BALTIMORE	13-Oct-95	13-Oct-95	03-Oct-95
NEW YORK	14-Oct-95	15-Oct-95	04-Oct-95
ALGECIRAS	23-Oct-95		16-Oct-95

FLY HOME FROM

EMERGENCY CONTACT

P&O Containers Fleet Personnel Department can be contacted by calling 0171-488-1313 or Freephone 0800 181 359. In extrememly urgent cases, after hours contact can be made by calling 0171-488-0047, you will be connected to the Duty Officer at his/her home telephone number.
An answer phone service giving details of ship movements and dates of anticipated crew changes is available on 0171-480-5889.
The ship can be contacted via the INMARSAT telephone system.
If the vessel is in the Atlantic or Mediterranean: phone 00 871 1440424
If the vessel is in the Indian Ocean :phone 00 873 1440424
If these numbers fail try also : 00 874 1440424 or 00 872 1440424.Calls are approx £6 per minute,so be prepared to leave the name of the person you wish to speak to and phone back in 5 minutes while he is contacted.

Alternatively, a telex message can be sent via the British Telecom public telex service,(details in phone book)or if you have access to a telex machine.
The ships U.K.telex no.is:94026294 KOWL G.This is an electronic mailbox and the ship may not get the telex for up to 12 hours. To send an immediate telex direct to the ship, phone 0800 378 398 and ask to send a telex via Portishead Radio,quoting ships satellite telex number: 1440424 GOYE

POSTAL ADDRESSES FOR CREW MAIL

ALGECIRAS
P+O CONTAINERS LTD,
c/o MARITIMA DEL MEDITERRANEO SA,
AVDA VIRGEN DEL CARMEN , 19C,
11201 ALGECIRAS,
CADIZ,
SPAIN

PORT SAID
NAGGAR SHIPPING COMPANY,
8 PALESTINE STREET,
P.O.BOX 450,
PORT SAID,
EGYPT

JEDDAH
P+O CONTAINERS DIVISION
PO BOX 7961,
4TH FLOOR ,KANDO CENTRE,
KILO 7,MEDINA ROAD,
JEDDAH 21472
SAUDI ARABIA

NHAVA SHEVA
M/S P+O(INDIAN AGENCIES) PVT LTD
PORT USERS BUILDING,
  2ND FLOOR
SHEVA TALUKA: URAN
RAIGAD DIST.,
NEW BOMBAY 400 707
INDIA

HALIFAX
P+O CONTAINERS
c/o PICKFORD + BLACK
P.O.BOX 1117,
HALIFAX,N.S.
B3J 2X1
CANADA

NEW YORK
P+O CONTAINERS
5080 MCLESTER STREET,
ELIZABETH,
NEW JERSEY 07201,
U.S.A

BALTIMORE
P+O CONTAINERS,
6610-B TRIBUTARY STREET,
  SUITE 101,
BALTIMORE,
MARYLAND 21224
U.S.A

CHARLESTON
C/O P+O CONTAINERS,
4055 FABER PLACE DRIVE,
SUITE 200,
N.CHARLESTON
SOUTH CAROLINA 29405,
U.S.A.

HOUSTON
P+O CONTAINERS,
1515 EAST BARBOURS CUT BLVD,
LAPORTE,
TEXAS 77571,
U.S.A

LONDON
FLEET MANAGAMENT DIVISION,
P+O CONTAINERS LTD,
BEAGLE HOUSE,
BRAHAM STREET,
LONDON E1 8EP
(Mark all letters:
  "CREW MAIL IN TRANSIT")

MARSAKLOKK(MALTA)
c/o CHARLES MUSU,
c/o THOMAS C.SMITH & CO.LTD,
12 ST.CHRISTOPHER ST,
VALLETTA,
MALTA.

SUEZ
NAGGAR SHIPPING COMPANY,
5 FANARAT + SAWAHEL STREET,
PO BOX 63,
PORT TEWFIK,
SUEZ
EGYPT

JEBEL ALI
P+O CONTAINERS LTD,
PO BOX 70,
AL RAS STREET,
DUBAI
UNITED ARAB EMIRATES

MIAMI
P+O CONTAINERS,
1800 ELLER DRIVE
  SUITE 318,
FORT LAUDERDALE,
FLORIDA 33316
U.S.A

PLEASE ENSURE ALL LETTERS
ARE ADDRESSED :
NAME,RANK/RATING,
M.V. KOWLOON BAY
FOLLOWED BY AGENTS ADDRESS

THE SEAMAN HE MUST HAVE THE SEA
THE ONLY LIFE HE KNOWS
HE IS ONLY HAPPY WHEN
LOOKING OUT ACROSS THE BOWS

THE SHIP IT IS HIS ONLY HOME
THE CREW HIS ONLY FAMILY
THE BOND THAT IS BETWEEN THEM
ON SHORE WOULD NEVER BE

THE WORLD IT IS HIS PLAYGROUND
EACH PORT A NEW PAGE IN HIS LIFE
THE LADIES THEY WILL ALLWAYS WELLCOME HIM
BUT NOWHERE WILL YOU FIND A WIFE

HE DOES NOT LOOK BACK WHEN LEAVING
WHERE HE'S BEEN, IS OF NO CONCERN
HE ONLY LOOKS TO WHAT IS AHEAD
NOT WHAT HE LEAVES ASTERN

EACH NIGHT IS LIKE A PICTURE SHOW
AS THE SUN SETS IN THE WEST
AND IF YOU ASK WHAT WAS HIS FAVOURITE
HE WILL SAY THE NEXT

THE SIGHTS THAT IS HAS SEEN
AND THE MEMORIES IN HIS MIND
IF HE HAD NOT GONE TO SEA
ON LAND HE WOULD NEVER FIND

AND ON THAT DAY
WHEN IS ANCHOR HE MUST LET GO
HE CAN LOOK BACK ON LIFE
FEW PEOPLE WILL EVER KNOW

RECEIVED

At   m.

By

POST OFFICE

TELEGRAM

Note—This form, together with the envelope in which it was delivered, should accompany any enquiry

| From | Prefix | Serial No. | Time handed in |

SENDER 437 1551 GRAYS T 14

= BOLTON 9 BOUNDARY ROAD

TO   FARM-HALEWOODLIVERPOOL26 =

| Sent at/by | Circulation |

PLEASE REPORT DOCK OFFICE 1500 WEDNESDAY

WITH GEAR = ELLIOTT +

9 26 + 1500 +   +TS 744/3

Don't speak to me of heroes until you've heard the tale
Of Britain's merchant seamen who sailed through storm and gale
To keep those lifelines open in our nations hour of need
When a tyrant cast a shadow across our island breed.
Captains, greasers, cabin boys, mates and engineers
Heard the call of duty and cast aside their fears.
While cooks and stewards manned the guns on coffins made of steel
They stoked those hungry boilers and stood behind the wheel.
They moved in icy convoys from Scapa to Murmansk
And crossed the western ocean, never seeking thanks.
They sailed the South Atlantic where raiders lay in wait
And kept the food lines open from Malta to the Cape.
Tracked by silent U-boats, which hunted from below.
Shelled by mighty cannons and fighters flying low,
They clung to burning lifeboats where the sea had turned to flame
And watched their shipmates disappear to ever lasting fame.
I speak not of a handful, but thirty thousand plus.
Some whose names we'll never know in whom we placed our trust.
They never knew the honour of medals on their chests,
Or marching bands and victory, glory and the rest.
The ocean is their resting place; their transport is the wind,
The seabirds cry their last goodbye to family and friend.
Freighters, troopships, liners and tankers by the score,
Fishing boats and coasters, two thousand ships and more
Flew the proud Red Duster as they sank beneath the waves,
And took those countless heroes to lonely ocean graves
Their legacy is freedom to those who hold it dear,
To walk with clear horizons and never hide in fear.
So when you talk of heroes remember those at sea,
From Britain's Merchant Navy who died to keep us free.

DATE AND PLACE OF BIRTH		NATIONALITY
25/1/47 *Sverten Lord*		*British*

	Colour of		
Height	Eyes	Hair	Complexion
5'3"	~~BLUE~~ BROWN	BLACK	FAIR

Tattoo or other Distinguishing Marks

~~NONE~~ TATTOOS BOTH ARMS.

Name, Relationship and Address of next-of-kin or nearest friend.

NAME *RUTH BOLTON*

RELATIONSHIP *MOTHER*

ADDRESS ~~138 GLOVETTA ROAD FORMBY~~
9, BOUNDARY FARM RD.,

CHANGE IN
ABOVE ADDRESS ~~~~ HALEWOOD,
LIVERPOOL 26.

ADDRESS OF SEAMAN
(if different from above)

CHANGE IN
SEAMAN'S ADDRESS

B.S.C. Serial No. *66367A*

SIGNATURE
OF SEAMAN } *EaBolton*

Appendix

List of ships and their companies I have sailed with and worked for:

Ship	Company
Buffalo	Link Line
Memestheus	Blue Funnel Line
Perseus	Blue Funnel Line
Norma	Transmarine
Beachwood	John I Jacobs
Samaria	Cunard Line
Ronsard	Lamport & Holt
Hinea	Shell Tanker
Adventura	Harrison Line
Swan River	Houlder Brothers
Newcastle Star	Blue Star
Doric	Shaw Savill
Northern Star	Shaw Savill
Persic	Shaw Savill
Empress Canada	Canadian Pacific
Silversand	Silver Line
Eastgate	Turnbel Scotts
Revaulx	Bolton Steam Ship
Ceramic	Shaw Savill
Cambria	British Rail
Canadian Star	Blue Star
Raeburn	Lamport & Holt
Columbia Star	Blue Star
California Star	Blue Star
New Zealand Star	Blue Star

Brazilia Star	Blue Star
Hobart Star	Blue Star
Afric Star	Blue Star
Hobart Star	Blue Star
Avelona Star	Blue Star
Ulster Star	Blue Star
California Star	Blue Star
Act I	Blue Star
Andalucia Star	Blue Star
Australia Star	Blue Star
Southland Star	Blue Star
Starman Anglia	Blue Star
Starman America	Blue Star
Boswell	Lamport & Holt
Ramgatira	Blue Star
Act 7	Blue Star
Scottish Star	Blue Star
English Star	Blue Star
British Reliance	BL Tanker
Dynamic Constructor	SBM UK
Maersk Neptune	Maersk Tanker
Maersk Nimrod	Maersk Tanker
Maersk Navarine	Maersk Tanker
Maersk Javelin	Maersk Tanker
Maersk Captian	Maersk Tanker
Maersk Gannett	Maersk Tanker
Pacific Swan	Fisher's Barrow
Maersk Anglia	Maersk Company
Consortium	NWW
Norse Lagan	Norse Irish Ferries
Norse Mersey	Norse Irish Ferries
Ned Lloyde Tasman	P&O Containers
Resolution Bay	P&O Containers
Jervis Bay	P&O Containers
Singapore Bay	P&O Containers
Peninsular Bay	P&O Containers

Repulse Bay	P&O Containers
Liverpool Bay	P&O Containers
Tokyo Bay	P&O Containers
Mairangi Bay	P&O Containers
Kowloon Bay	P&O Containers
Far Turbot	Farstad
Far Scotsman	Farstad
White Thorn	James Fisher
Komander Subsea	Hays Ships
Amersham	Maersk Ships
Apricity	Everards
Charles Darwin	RUS Marine
Hornbeck Castor	Tidewater
Maersk Beater	Maersk Company
Norskald	DSNU Survey
Nexus	James Fisher
Global Mariner	ITF
Viking Viper	Viking Ships
Pacific Bammer	Swires
Neptumia	POR Valetta
Oceanic Cavalier	James Fisher
Fisher Cavalier	James Fisher
Sefton Supporter	GSM Ltd
European Pathfinder	P&O Ferries
Sand Serim	South Coast Shipping
Mercury Bay	Gulf Offshore
Arco Humber	Hansons
Grampian Shield	North Star Shipping
RS Ernest Shackleton	RRS
Pacific Blade	Swires
Pacific Blade	Swires
Pacific Blade	Swires
Pacific Blade	Swires
Pacific Blade	Swires
Pacific Blade	Swires
Pacific Barbarian	Swires

Wave Ruler	Royal Fleet Aux
Highland Eagle	Gulf Offshore
UK Dolphin	UK Dredging
UK Dolphin	UK Dredging
Hartland Point	Bibbys
Hartland Point	Bibbys
Anvil Point	Bibbys
Anvil Point	Bibbys
Border Heather	BP Shipping
Anvil Point	Bibbys
Sand Harrier	RMC Marine
Arco Aron	Hansons
Hartland Point	Bibbys
Hurst Point	Bibbys
Alo Adur	Hansons
Medway	Westminster Dredging
Mina	Scottish Fisheries
Highland Piper	Gulf Offshore
Sand Falcon	Cemex
Hurst Point	Bibbys
Sand Falcon	Cemex
Eddystone	Bibbys
Dolphin	UK Dredging
Anvil Point	Bibbys
Hurst Point	Bibbys
Hurst Point	Bibbys
Gargano	Gulf Offshore
Hurst Point	Bibbys
Hartland Point	Bibbys
Hartland Point	Bibbys
Ocean Spey	Sarta Offshore
Longstone	Bibbys
Hurst Point	Bibbys
Bibby Tethira	Osirus Projects
ASV Pioneer	Barge
Cefas Endeavour	P&O

Hurst Point	Bibbys
Grampian Otter	North Star
Grampian Otter	North Star
Caledonian Vanguard	Bibbys
Ocean West	Atlantic Offshore
Ocean Cleaver	Atlantic Offshore
Ocean Swan	Atlantic Offshore
Arco Beck	Hansons
Arco Aron	Hansons
Arco Dee	Hansons
Arco Beck	Hansons
UKD Bluefin	UKD Dredging
Arco Beck	Hansons
Pegasus	Fletcher Shipping
LM Constructor	Land & Marine
Balmoral	Fletcher Supply
Arco Dijk	Hansons

Printed in Great Britain
by Amazon